MCQs World History Quiz Book

Yasir Bashir

More than 1,200 multiple choice questions

Table of Contents

Quiz No 1

1. Who was the first sultan of Egypt and Syria, and the founder of the Ayyubid dynasty?
   a. Al-Ashraf Musa
   b. Al-Kamil
   c. Salahuddin
   d. Al-Adil

2. Which crusade was led by the new king of England, Richard the Lionheart?
   a. Third crusade
   b. First crusade
   c. Second crusade
   d. Fourth crusade

3. In which city can you find the buildings which reflect the dominance of Roman, Byzantine, early Muslim, Christian crusader, Ayyubid and Mamluk Muslim, Ottoman, and modern powers rulers?
   a. Cairo
   b. Jerusalem
   c. Athens
   d. Damascus

4. Which Roman prefect is best known for ordering the Crucifixion of Jesus?
   a. Publius Octavius
   b. Aelius Gallus
   c. Marcus Aurelius

d.   Pontius Pilate

5. When the whole world used to be joined in one super-continent, what was that super-continent called?
   a.   Pangaea
   b.   Sirius
   c.   Arcturus
   d.   Rigel

6. How long ago was Britain actually connected to continent Europe by land?
   a.   100,000 years ago
   b.   200,000 years ago
   c.   800,000 years ago
   d.   450,000 years ago

7. Which of the following is one of Seven Wonders of the Ancient World?
   a.   Christ the Redeemer
   b.   Great Pyramid of Giza
   c.   Taj Mahal
   d.   Machu Picchu

8. Which of the following places has made Orkney a magnet for archaeologists, historians and researchers?
   a.   Battle Abbey
   b.   Maiden castle
   c.   Ness of Brodgar
   d.   Stonehenge

9. Which of the following instruments are normally used to carry out geophysical surveys to pinpoint manmade artefacts hidden underground?
   a.   Magnetometers
   b.   Ground-penetrating radars

     c.   Light Detection and Ranging (LIDAR)

     d.   All of the above

10. When did the first domestication of animals take place in Central Asia?

     a.   9,500 years ago

     b.   105,00 years ago

     c.   500 years ago

     d.   5,500 years ago

Answers Quiz 1

1. (c) Sultan Salahuddin Ayubi (1137-1193)
2. (a) Third crusade
3. (b) Jerusalem
4. (d) Pontius Pilate
5. (a) Pangaea
6. (d) About half a million years ago (450,000)
7. (b) Great Pyramid of Giza
8. (c) Ness of Brodgar
9. (d) All of the above
10. (d) 5,500 years ago

Quiz No 2

1. According to existing theory, when was domestication of horses and evolution of culture took place?

     a.   In the late Paleolithic period

     b.   In the late Mesolithic period

     c.   In the late Neolithic period

d.   In the late Chalcolithic period

2.   When did the latest Ice Age come to an end?
a.   Around 10,000 years ago
b.   Around 5500 years ago
c.   Around 20,000 years ago
d.   Around 50,000 years ago

3.   When did Britain become separated from the European mainland?
a.   Shortly before 10,000BC
b.   Shortly before 1,000BC
c.   Shortly before 6,000BC
d.   Shortly before 3,000BC

4.   What is widely regarded as one of the biggest changes in human history?
a.   Introduction of tools
b.   Introduction of horses
c.   Introduction of castles
d.   Introduction of farming

5.   Because of being situated at one of the world's main cross-roads, civilization developed early in which of these regions of the world?
a.   South-East Asia
b.   Western Asia
c.   Eastern Asia
d.   Sub-Saharan Africa

6.   Which communities didn't encourage a more settled way of life and moved around Britain on a seasonal pattern, following the animals, birds and fish they hunted?
a.   Mesolithic

      b.   Neolithic

      c.   Middle Neolithic

      d.   Chalcolithic

7. Where in the world were the first seed grain of wheat and barley bred from wild grasses were grown?

      a.   Sub-Saharan Africa

      b.   Modern-day Iraq

      c.   Eurasia

      d.   Central Asia

8. Which of the following is the usually accepted start date for Bronze Age?

      a.   5500 BC

      b.   4500 BC

      c.   2500 BC

      d.   3500 BC

9. Which of the following are the first great civilizations?

      a.   Egyptian

      b.   Mesopotamian

      c.   Indus Valley

      d.   All of the above

10. What is the land between the Tigris and Euphrates rivers, commonly known by its Greek name?

      a.   South-East Asia

      b.   Middle East

      c.   Central Asia

      d.   Mesopotamia

Answers Quiz 2

1. (c) In the late Neolithic period
2. (a) Around 10,000 years ago
3. (c) Shortly before 6,000BC
4. (d) Introduction of farming
5. (a) South-East Asia
6. (a) Mesolithic
7. (b) Modern-day Iraq
8. (c) 2500 BC
9. (d) All of the above
10. (d) Mesopotamia

Quiz No 3

1. Where did Indus Valley civilization, one of the first great civilizations, flourish?
   a. Turkey
   b. Pakistan
   c. Egypt
   d. Mexico

2. All three first great civilizations, Egyptian, Mesopotamian and Indus Valley, had which of the following common features?
   a. Complex health systems
   b. Complex education systems
   c. Complex transport systems
   d. Complex irrigation systems

3. When did the Greek historian Herodotus visit Egypt?
   a. In the 5th century BC
   b. In the 6th century BC
   c. In the 2nd century BC

d.   In the 3rd century BC

4.   Sigmund Freud is the author of which of the following books?
   a.   The Iliad and the Odyssey
   b.   Republic
   c.   Moses and Monotheism
   d.   Critique of Pure Reason

5.   Emergence of which of these does mark the start of a new phase of world history?
   a.   Oceanic voyages
   b.   Migration from villages to cities
   c.   End of Ice ages
   d.   First civilizations

6.   Choose True or False: The early civilizations of America arose a little later than the first civilizations?
   a.   True
   b.   False
   c.   All of the above
   d.   None of the above

7.   Statue of which of the following pharaohs was designed to show him as beneficent ruler, a mighty ruler, and a living god?
   a.   Ramesses II
   b.   Djoser
   c.   Thutmose III
   d.   Amenhotep III

8.   Who built the Great Temple of Abu Simbel in 1257 BC?
   a.   Khufu
   b.   Tutankhamun

        c.   Djoser
        d.   Rameses II

9. Where do the earliest known hominine fossils come
        from that is 4.5 million years old?
        a.   Afar region of Ethiopia
        b.   Middle East
        c.   South-East Asia
        d.   Southeastern region of Mexico

10. Where were the earliest-known stone tools found which
        are 2.5 million years old?
        a.   Jerusalem, Israel
        b.   Gona, Ethiopia
        c.   Mesopotamia, Turkey
        d.   Cairo, Egypt

Answers Quiz 3

1. (b) Pakistan
2. (d) Complex irrigation systems
3. (a) In the 5th century BC
4. (c) Moses and Monotheism
5. (d) First civilizations
6. (b) False (The early civilizations of America arose
        considerably later)
7. (a) Pharaoh Ramesses II
8. (d) King Rameses II
9. (a) Afar region of Ethiopia
10. (b) Gona, Ethiopia

Quiz No 4

1. Which of these is best known from the Nariokotome skeleton?
    a. Homo ergaster
    b. Homo sapiens
    c. Homo erectus
    d. Homo heidelbergensis

2. How long ago was Australia reached by boat?
    a. By 20,000 years
    b. By 10,000 years
    c. By 5,000 years
    d. By 50,000 years

3. How long ago did humans begin to settle the deep Pacific islands?
    a. About 12,000 years
    b. About 8,000 years
    c. About 2,000 years
    d. About 10,000 years

4. Humans had reached New Zealand 1,000 years before the island was discovered by whom?
    a. Ibn Battuta
    b. Ernest Shackleton
    c. Captain Cook
    d. Marco Polo

5. Which of the following were the first anatomically modern humans?
    a. Homo ergaster
    b. Homo sapiens
    c. Homo erectus

        d.   Homo floresiensis

6. How many have there been Ice Ages in the last 800,000 years?
- a. 8
- b. 2
- c. 6
- d. 5

7. When did the last Ice Age end?
- a. 10,000 years ago
- b. 50,000 years ago
- c. 30,000 years ago
- d. 20,000 years ago

8. When were the Neanderthals drawn to extinction?
- a. 10,000 years ago
- b. 20,000 years ago
- c. 15,000 years ago
- d. 25,000 years ago

9. What does remain among the most potent and vivid images created by the artists of the late Ice Age in Europe?
- a. Lion
- b. Bison
- c. Mammoth
- d. Snake

10. In which of the following centuries did the Heptarchy, seven separate Anglo-Saxon kingdoms, emerge in England?
- a. In the 3rd century
- b. In the 9th century
- c. In the 7th century

d.   In the 5th century

Answers Quiz 4

1. (a) Homo Ergaster
2. (d) By 50,000 years
3. (c) About 2,000 years
4. (c) Captain Cook
5. (b) *Homo sapiens*
6. (a) 8
7. (a) 10,000 years ago, 10,000 BC
8. (d) 25,000 years ago, or 25,000 BC
9. (b) Bison from the caves at Altamira, near Santander in northern Spain
10. (c) In the 7th century

Quiz No 5

1. Until 8,000 years ago, humankind consisted of which of these?
    a.   Bands of Hunters and Gatherers
    b.   Bands of Vikings
    c.   Bands of Egyptians
    d.   Bands of Babylonians

2. Where did in the world new lifestyles begin to develop based on cultivation rather than collecting plant foods?
    a.   China
    b.   West Asia
    c.   Sub-Saharan Africa

d.   Central America

3. When did rice cultivation begin in South China?
    a.   About 1,000 BC
    b.   About 2,000 BC
    c.   About 8,000 BC
    d.   About 6,000 BC

4. Which of the following parts of the globe especially had contributed to the earliest domestication of plants and animals?
    a.   Those between 20° South and 30° North
    b.   Those between 30° South and 400° North
    c.   Those between 15° South and 35° North
    d.   Those between 10° South and 50° North

5. When did the Roman emperor Heraclius defeat Persia and captured the Nineveh?
    a.   AD 610
    b.   AD 628
    c.   AD 600
    d.   AD 650

6. Which of the following religions initiated as a splinter of Judaism, but the followers turned instead to the conversion of non-Jews?
    a.   Hinduism
    b.   Jainism
    c.   Christianity
    d.   Buddhism

7. Where had been the earliest and most important centres of cereal cultivation?
    a.   South-West Asia
    b.   Middle East

    c. South Africa

    d. Eurasia

8. When was the climate in the Sahara much more
   favourable than today?
       a. Between 7,000 BC and 4,000 BC
       b. Between 9,000 BC and 3,000 BC
       c. Between 5,000 BC and 1,000 BC
       d. Between 6,000 BC and 2,000 BC

9. How can you find a connection between deserts of the
   Kalahari and central Australia, rainforests of Amazon
   basin, central Africa and South-East Asia, and in the
   Arctic?
       a. Surviving representatives of Byzantine empire
          are found only there
       b. Surviving representatives of Egyptian
          pharaohs are found only there
       c. Surviving representatives of hunters and
          gatherers are found only there
       d. Surviving representatives of Viking people are
          found only there

10. What was the world population in 15,000 BC?
       a. 150 million
       b. 50 million
       c. 10 million
       d. 100 million

Answers Quiz 5

1. (a) Bands of Hunters and Gatherers
2. (a) (b) China and West Asia

3. (d) About 6,000 BC
4. (d) Those between 10° South and 50° North
5. (b) AD 628
6. (c) Christianity
7. (a) South-West Asia
8. (b) Between 9,000 BC and 3,000 BC
9. (c) Surviving representatives of hunters and gatherers are found only there
10. (c) 10 million

Quiz No 6

1. What was the world population in AD 1,500?
    a.   50 million
    b.   300 million
    c.   500 million
    d.   350 million

2. Before Islamic era, which state arose to prominence in Africa?
    a.   Ghana
    b.   Nigeria
    c.   South Africa
    d.   Somalia

3. The first economies were based on which of these?
    a.   Hunting
    b.   Killing & plundering
    c.   Animal husbandry
    d.   Plant staples

4. When were the first sheep domesticated in Mesopotamia?
   a. Around 4000 BC
   b. Around 5000 BC
   c. Around 9000 BC
   d. Around 1000 BC

5. When was Alfred the Great of Wessex ruler in England?
   a. Between 971 and 999
   b. Between 671 and 699
   c. Between 771 and 799
   d. Between 871 and 899

6. When did developed Neolithic villages come into being?
   a. Around 7,000 and 6,000 BC
   b. Around 8,000 and 7,000 BC
   c. Around 6,000 and 5,000 BC
   d. Around 4,000 and 3,000 BC

7. When did bronze working in Thailand and Vietnam start?
   a. Around 1800 BC
   b. Around 1500 BC
   c. Around 800 BC
   d. Around 1000 BC

8. Which of these is the first fortified settlement in the world?
   a. Pompeii, Italy
   b. Cairo, Egypt
   c. Petra, Jordan
   d. Jericho, Palestine

9. From its creation, to which of the following sides was the centre of gravity of the Roman empire shifted?
    a. Eastern
    b. Western
    c. Southern
    d. Northern

10. Where were the ox-drawn ploughs first used?
    a. Middle East
    b. South Asia
    c. Eurasia
    d. Sub-Saharan

Answers Quiz 6

1. (d) 350 million
2. (a) Ghana
3. (c) (d) Animal husbandry and plant staples
4. (c) Around 9000 BC
5. (d) Between 871 and 899
6. (a) Around 7,000 and 6,000 BC
7. (b) Around 1500 BC
8. (d) Jericho, Palestine
9. (a) Eastern
10. (c) Eurasia

Quiz No 7

1. Why were the farming communities grew bigger and differentiated than hunter-gatherers?

a. Because cultivated crops provided the food all year round
b. Because cultivated food was stored for a longer duration
c. Because farming people needed to stay close to their crops
d. All of the above

2. When were the first cities developed?
   a. Around 6,000 BC
   b. Around 3,000 BC
   c. Around 5,000 BC
   d. Around 8,000 BC

3. Epipalaeolithic period refers to which of these?
   a. 12,000-9,000 BC
   b. 10,000-8,000 BC
   c. 7,000-4,000 BC
   d. 15,000-10,000 BC

4. Which of these was a Byzantine emperor between 976 and 1025?
   a. Alexios I
   b. Constantine IV
   c. Basil II
   d. Heraclius

5. Followers of which of the following religions consist of one-seventh of the global population?
   a. Islam
   b. Christianity
   c. Hinduism
   d. Buddhism

6. What are the seven separate Anglo-Saxon kingdoms, which rose in England in the 7th century, known as?
- a. Septemviral
- b. Septennial
- c. Heptarchy
- d. Septinary

7. In Mesopotamia, when were the cities persisted?
- a. About 4,500 BC
- b. About 3,500 BC
- c. About 2,500 BC
- d. About 1,500 BC

8. What did the founder of the Christianity, Jesus of Nazareth, claim to be?
- a. Messiah
- b. Reverent
- c. Pious
- d. Dedicated

9. When did German king Otto 1 defeat the Magyars of Hungary at the Lechfeld?
- a. AD 755
- b. AD 855
- c. AD 955
- d. AD 1055

10. When was the New World (the Americas) captured by Europeans?
- a. After 1492
- b. After 1392
- c. After 1592
- d. After 1692

Answers Quiz 7

1. (d) All of the above
2. (b) Around 3,000 BC
3. (a) Between 12,000 and 9,000 BC
4. (c) Basil II
5. (a) Islam
6. (c) Heptarchy
7. (b) About 3,500 BC
8. (a) The Messiah or Saviour
9. (c) AD 955
10. (a) After 1492

Quiz No 8

1. Where did the first civilizations emerge?
   a. From the basin of four major rivers: Tigris and Euphrates, the Nile, Yellow River and Indus
   b. Central African states: Angola, Chad, Congo and Rwanda
   c. Countries bordering the Atlantic Ocean: United Kingdom, United States, Russia and South Africa
   d. Landlocked countries: Kazakhstan, Uzbekistan, Afghanistan and Switzerland

2. When did cities already exist in Egypt?
   a. By 2200 BC
   b. By 1200 BC
   c. By 3200 BC
   d. By 4200 BC

3. Choose true or false: The earliest writings were used for the purpose of keeping the record of commodities, wages and taxes but soon later used as a means of registering religious traditions, social customs and myths?
   a. True
   b. False

4. Where were the first trading centres developed?
   a. Eastern Mediterranean, Indus Valley and China
   b. Eurasia, Central Asia and Americas
   c. Europe, Central Africa and South Africa
   d. Southern America, North Africa and Russia

5. When did Arabs launch two long sieges of Byzantium which ended in failure?
   a. Between 874-78 and 917-18
   b. Between 774-78 and 817-18
   c. Between 574-78 and 617-18
   d. Between 674-78 and 717-18

6. During the 6th century BC, principal preachers and reformers of which of the following religions lived?
   a. Christianity, Zoroastrianism, Diasporic
   b. Islam, Jainism, Shinto, Tenrikyo and Bahai
   c. Hinduism, Buddhism, Judaism, Confucianism and Taoism
   d. Sikhism, Spiritism, Juche and Neo-Paganism

7. When were the first civilizations of the Americas developed?
   a. Around 500 BC
   b. Around 1,500 BC

c.   Around 3,500 BC

d.   Around 2,500 BC

8.   When was the Shang dynasty developed in China?
   a.   By 800 BC
   b.   By 3,800 BC
   c.   By 2,800 BC
   d.   By 1,800 BC

9.   The Royal Standard of Ur which is the largest of the royal tombs at Ur. What does it show?
   a.   Scenes of natural beauty
   b.   Scenes of peace and war
   c.   Scenes of flourishing civilization
   d.   Scenes of complex irrigation and sewage system

10.   In Africa, which empire developed around Lake Chad and the Hausa city states?
   a.   Achaemenid
   b.   Hittite
   c.   Kanum-Borneo
   d.   Assyrian

Answers Quiz 8

1.   (a) From the basin of four major rivers: Tigris and Euphrates in Mesopotamia, the Nile in Egypt, Yellow River in China, and Indus in Pakistan

2.   (c) By 3200 BC

3.   (a) True: To keep the record of commodities, wages and taxes but soon later used as a mean of registering religious traditions, social customs and myths

4. (a) Eastern Mediterranean, Indus Valley and China

5. (d) Between 674-78 and 717-18

6. (c) Hinduism, Buddhism, Judaism, Confucianism and Taoism

7. (b) Around 1,500 BC

8. (d) By 1,800 BC

9. (b) Scenes of peace and war

10. (c) Kanum-Borneo

Quiz No 9

1. Where can you visit one of the Seven Wonders of the Ancient World, the Great Pyramid of Giza?
   a. Jordan
   b. Turkey
   c. Egypt
   d. Syria

2. The earliest of all known civilizations, Sumer, consisted of how many cities in northern Mesopotamia?
   a. Some 3 city-states
   b. Some 2 city-states
   c. Some 15 city-states
   d. Some 12 city-states

3. Under Charles IV (1333-78) which region made significant progress in Europe?
   a. Bohemia
   b. Germany
   c. Iceland
   d. Ireland

4. When did the first powerful leaders occupy over vast areas?

    a.   By 2,000 BC

    b.   By 3,000 BC

    c.   By 1,000 BC

    d.   By 5,000 BC

5. When was the period of 'Old Kingdom' in Egypt?

    a.   Between 4685 and 4180 BC

    b.   Between 2685 and 2180 BC

    c.   Between 1685 and 1180 BC

    d.   Between 3685 and 3180 BC

6. When were all the major powers of the Eastern Mediterranean invaded by the 'Sea Peoples' and 'Dark Age' commenced?

    a.   About 1,200 BC

    b.   About 300 BC

    c.   About 1000 BC

    d.   About 200 BC

7. Where did the Aztec Empire flourish?

    a.   Peru

    b.   Mexico

    c.   Turkey

    d.   Israel

8. When was Tiglath-pileser III the king?

    a.   Between 544 and 527 BC

    b.   Between 644 and 627 BC

    c.   Between 744 and 727 BC

    d.   Between 444 and 427 BC

9. Who were the successors of the Babylonian empire?

    a.   Persians

b. Pharaohs

c. Mongols

d. Aztecs

10. When did the last pharaoh of Egypt, Rameses III, die?

    a. 120 BC

    b. 3,120 BC

    c. 2,120 BC

    d. 1,120 BC

Answers Quiz 9

1. (c) Egypt

2. (d) Some 12 city-states

3. (a) Bohemia

4. (b) By 3,000 BC

5. (b) Between 2685 and 2180 BC

6. (a) About 1,200 BC

7. (b) Mexico

8. (c) Between 744 and 727 BC

9. (a) Persians

10. (d) 1,120 BC

Quiz No 10

1. Which of the following pharaohs died in 1,120 BC?

    a. Djoser

    b. Tutankhamun

    c. Khufu

    d. Rameses III

2. Babylonian empire was overrun by whom in 539 BC?

    a.   Romans

    b.   Mongols

    c.   Persians

    d.   Aztecs

3. Which of the following were the early empires of Mesopotamia?

    a.   Sumerian settlement

    b.   Empire of Agade

    c.   III Ur empire

    d.   Empire of Hammurabi

    e.   All of the above

4. When did the Mongols overthrow the Abbasid Caliphate?

    a.   Between 256 and 260

    b.   Between 1256 and 1260

    c.   Between 3256 and 3260

    d.   Between 2256 and 2260

5. What is known as the Old Kingdom Egypt?

    a.   Between 2,685 and 2,180 BC

    b.   Between 4,685 and 4,180 BC

    c.   Between 1,685 and 1,180 BC

    d.   Between 3,685 and 3,180 BC

6. When was the reign of Abbas the Great, which was the apogee of Safavid empire?

    a.   Between 1587 and 1629

    b.   Between 1287 and 1329

    c.   Between 1387 and 1429

    d.   Between 1487 and 1529

7. From Asia, the people migrated to the Americas and colonized them late in the last Ice Age. How did that happen?
    a. As Bering Strait was a dry land due to lowered sea levels
    b. As all continents were together known as Pangaea
    c. As Asia and Americas were very close
    d. As people had developed ships

8. Which victories left the Turks masters of the Balkans?
    a. Kosovo
    b. Nicopolis
    c. Romania
    d. Greece

9. Where was the cultivation of Maize, beans and squash spread to North America?
    a. Mexico
    b. Peru
    c. Brazil
    d. Paraguay

10. In England, whose determined resistance held the Danes at bay?
    a. Alfred the Great of Wessex
    b. King Henry VIII
    c. William of Normandy
    d. William of Orange

Answers Quiz 10

1. (d) Last pharaoh of Egypt, Rameses III

2. (c) Persians
3. (e) All of the above
4. (b) Between 1256 and 1260
5. (a) Between 2,685 and 2,180 BC
6. (a) Between 1587 and 1629
7. (a) As Bering Strait was a dry land due to lowered sea levels
8. (a) (b) Kosovo and Nicopolis
9. (a) Mexico
10. (a) Alfred the Great of Wessex (871-99)

Quiz No 11

1. What was one of the most important aspects for the initiation of a period of rapid development in North America?
   a. Flourishing of Aztec empire
   b. Cultivation of maize, beans and squash
   c. Development of Mayan civilization
   d. Byzantium warriors reached in Mexico

2. Which of these were powerful lowland kingdoms that became prosperous around AD 100?
   a. Babylonian
   b. Inca
   c. Maya
   d. Aztec

3. Why were most of the towns of the Maya kingdoms abandoned between AD 790 and 860?
   a. Constant wars
   b. Popular discontent

     c.   Degradation of environmental due to increase in population

     d.   All of the above

4. When did the Mongol empire establish in one way or the other on the world map?
- a. Between 1406 and 1896
- b. Between 1306 and 1796
- c. Between 1206 and 1696
- d. Between 1006 and 1596

5. When did the first Viking invade England?
- a. 793
- b. 993
- c. 693
- d. 893

6. Which of the following civilizations were established in the Classic period - between AD 300 and 800 - in Mesoamerica?
- a. Teotihuacan civilization
- b. Classic Gulf coast civilization
- c. Zapotec civilization
- d. Maya civilization
- e. All of the above

7. When did Australia become separated by sea from the rest of the Old World?
- a. About 20,000 years ago
- b. About 5000 years ago
- c. About 15,000 years ago
- d. About 10,000 years ago

8. When were the first settlers reached Melanesian islands from New Guinea?

a.   About 100 BC
b.   About 1,300 BC
c.   About 1000 BC
d.   About 300 BC

9.   When was Louis the Pious the emperor of the whole Carolingian dynasty in Europe?
a.   Between 914 and 940
b.   Between 614 and 640
c.   Between 814 and 840
d.   Between 714 and 740

10.   Who were the Mongols?
a.   A nomadic people from the grasslands of Central Asia
b.   A nomadic people from the grasslands of South Africa
c.   A nomadic people from the grasslands of Northern Europe
d.   A nomadic people from the grasslands of Central Europe

Answers Quiz 11

1.   (b) Cultivation of maize, beans and squash
2.   (c) Mayan
3.   (d) All of the above
4.   (c) Between 1206 and 1696
5.   (a) 793
6.   (e) All of the above
7.   (c) About 10,000 years ago
8.   (b) About 1,300 BC
9.   (c) Between 814 and 840

10. (a) A nomadic people from the grasslands of Central Asia

Quiz No 12

1. When were the Hawaii islands first colonized?
    a.   Around AD 300
    b.   Around AD 600
    c.   Around AD 500
    d.   Around AD 400

2. When did Portuguese first arrive in the south-east and south-west coasts of Africa?
    a.   Near the end of the 15th century
    b.   Near the end of the 12th century
    c.   Near the end of the 13th century
    d.   Near the end of the 17th century

3. When did rock art emerge in Australia which was commonly found marking the sacred places of Aborigines?
    a.   Around 7,000 ago
    b.   Around 10,000 ago
    c.   Around 25,000 ago
    d.   Around 5,000 ago

4. When was the Sahara Desert emerged due to desiccation?
    a.   Between 6,000 and 5,000 BC
    b.   Between 2,000 and 1,000 BC
    c.   Between 4,000 and 3,000 BC
    d.   Between 3,000 and 2,000 BC

5. When did the Kingdom of Meroe arise?
- a. By 300 BC
- b. By 900 BC
- c. By 700 BC
- d. By 500 BC

6. What do Panaramitee engravings, complex figurative, and simple figurative share in common?
- a. Rock art styles of first settlers of Polynesia and island Micronesia
- b. Rock art styles of first settlers of Australia
- c. Rock art styles of first settlers of Americas
- d. Rock art styles of first settlers of Africa

7. When did the initial settlements in Eastern Polynesia establish?
- a. Between 10 BC and AD 1500
- b. Between 500 BC and AD 5000
- c. Between 150 BC and AD 1,000
- d. Between 1500 BC and AD 100

8. Where was the first great Indian civilization established in the 3rd millennium?
- a. Indus Valley
- b. Himalayan Mountains
- c. Eastern Pakistan
- d. Northern India

9. Who was the founder of the teachings of Jainism?
- a. Mahavira
- b. Jesus of Nazareth
- c. Muhammad
- d. Buddha

10. Choose True or False: The Aztec and Inca Empires differed markedly in character and no contact existed between them?
    a. True
    b. False
    c. All of the above
    d. None of the above

Answers Quiz 12

1. (d) Around AD 400
2. (a) Near the end of the 15th century
3. (c) Around 25,000 ago
4. (c) Between 4,000 and 3,000 BC
5. (b) By 900 BC
6. (a) Rock art styles of first settlers of Polynesia and island Micronesia
7. (c) Between 150 BC and AD 1,000
8. (b) Indus Valley
9. (a) Mahavira
10. (a) True

Quiz No 13

1. When was rice first cultivated in the subcontinent?
    a. Around 1,000 BC
    b. Around 3,000 BC
    c. Around 5,000 BC
    d. Around 7,000 BC

2. Bronze Dong Son drums date back to…?

     a.   Around 7,000 BC

     b.   Around 5,000 BC

     c.   Around 3,000 BC

     d.   Around 1,000 BC

3. When were the Hindu temples built in Burma, Cambodia and Java?

     a.   Around AD 900

     b.   Around AD 100

     c.   Around AD 700

     d.   Around AD 500

4. After the Gandhara state invasion, in present-day north-western Pakistan, by Alexander the Great, it was conquered by whom?

     a.   Maurya

     b.   Mamluk

     c.   Lodhi

     d.   Khilji

5. When was Gautama Buddha, founder of Buddhism, born?

     a.   486 BC

     b.   AD 486

     c.   786 BC

     d.   AD 786

6. When was farming expanded from West Asia to Europe?

     a.   Around 3,500 BC

     b.   Around 6,500 BC

     c.   Around 4,500 BC

     d.   Around 5,500 BC

7. From its emergence, why did the Roman empire's centre of gravity shift to the east?
    a. Due to economic wealth in Egypt and western Asia
    b. Due to fall of its western provinces at the hands of Germanic invaders
    c. Due to the pressure of Sassanid Persia on its eastern frontier
    d. All of the above

8. With the development of labour-intensive sugar-plantations in the Americas which of the following trades developed and attracted others?
    a. Slave
    b. Spice
    c. Shipping
    d. Diamond

9. Who was a charismatic leader of the Mongols, who was born in 1167 and died 1227?
    a. Kublai Khan
    b. Guyuk Khan
    c. Temujin
    d. Timur Khan

10. Which of these was the dominant process for the emergence of agricultural communities in Europe?
    a. Adoption of agriculture by existing populations
    b. Expansion of colonizing populations
    c. Onslaughts of Vikings
    d. Onslaughts of Mongols

Answers Quiz 13

1. (b) Around 3,000 BC
2. (d) Around 1,000 BC
3. (c) Around AD 700
4. (a) Maurya empire
5. (a) 486 BC
6. (b) Around 6,500 BC
7. (d) All of the above
8. (a) Slave
9. (c) Temujin also known as Genghis Khan
10. (a) Adoption of agriculture by existing populations

Quiz No 14

1. When did copper-working come into use in Europe?
    a. Around 1,500 BC
    b. Around 2,500 BC
    c. Around 4,500 BC
    d. Around 3,500 BC

2. Which of the following was the earliest state of Europe?
    a. Crete
    b. Mycenae
    c. Bohemia
    d. Kent

3. In Homer's Iliad which of these has been described?
    a. Battle of Mohacs
    b. Trojan War

     c.   Reformation

     d.   Enlightenment

4. Followers of which of the following religions consist of almost 600 million of the global population?

     a.   Islam

     b.   Jainism

     c.   Judaism

     d.   Hinduism

5. When were the first farming communities established in Europe?

     a.   Around 500 BC

     b.   Around 2,500 BC

     c.   Around 4,500 BC

     d.   Around 6,500 BC

6. Which two major civilizations confronted the Spaniards when they arrived on the American mainland in the early 16th century?

     a.   Achaemenid

     b.   Assyrian

     c.   Aztec

     d.   Inca

7. During the 8th century BC, the Phoenician exploration and settlement were the most prominent on which of the following islands?

     a.   Rhodes

     b.   Euboea

     c.   Chryse

     d.   Jordsand

8. By the end of the first millennium AD, where was the rise of a culture based on iron-working led to the appearance of extensive states and empires based on trade?

    a.   North America

    b.   South America

    c.   Asia

    d.   Africa

9. After the fall of the Mycenaean palace system, which of these was arisen as the prominent form of political organisation in the Mediterranean?

    a.   Polis

    b.   Whig

    c.   Tory

    d.   Federalist

10. Which of these is a prime Greek sculptor, painter and artist?

    a.   Michelangelo

    b.   El Greco

    c.   Phidias

    d.   Pablo Picasso

Answers Quiz 14

1. (c) Around 4,500 BC

2. (a) Crete

3. (b) Trojan War

4. (a) Islam

5. (d) Around 6,500 BC

6. (c) (d) Aztec Empire in Mexico & Inca Empire in Peru

7. (b) Euboea

8. (d) Africa

9. (a) Polis or city-state

10. (c) Phidias

Quiz No 15

1. After the collapse of the Mycenaean empire in 1,200 BC which of these followed for four centuries?
    a. Ice Age
    b. Dark Age
    c. Achaemenid Empire
    d. Assyrian Empire

2. Which of the following centuries was a period of great evolution in Greece?
    a. The 2nd century BC
    b. The 4th century BC
    c. The 6th century BC
    d. The 8th century BC

3. When did the Persians invade Greece and met with defeat?
    a. 180-179 BC
    b. 280-279 BC
    c. 480-479 BC
    d. 380-379 BC

4. When was Athens executed expedition against Syracuse of Sicily which proved disastrously straining of its resources?
    a. Between 15 and 13 BC
    b. Between 215 and 213 BC
    c. Between 615 and 613 BC
    d. Between 415 and 413 BC

5. When was Ming China the most powerful and advanced state of the world with over 100 million inhabitants?

    a. In the 11th century
    b. In the 12th century
    c. In the 16th century
    d. In the 15th century

6. Under whose leadership a well-trained Macedonian army was created and led an attack on Persia?

    a. Philip II
    b. Nero
    c. Yang of Sui
    d. Genghis Khan

7. When did the Mongol invasion in the south of China take place, when much of the land went out of cultivation, many cities and industries perished, and countless people died or became slaves?

    a. Between 1071 and 1079
    b. Between 1271 and 1279
    c. Between 1571 and 1579
    d. Between 271 and 279

8. Whose leading generals created the important powers of Macedon, Egypt and the Seleucid kingdom of western Asia?

    a. Umar Ibn Khattab
    b. Caligula
    c. Alexander the Great
    d. Genghis Khan

9. When was Greek colonization prominent in the Mediterranean world?

a. Between 550 and 350 BC
b. Between 950 and 750 BC
c. Between 350 and 50 BC
d. Between 750 and 550 BC

10. When was the capital of the east Roman empire sacked by the Ottoman Turks and the Byzantine empire totally crumbled?
a. 1453
b. 1483
c. 1453
d. 1435

Answers Quiz 15

1. (b) Dark Age
2. (d) The 8th century BC
3. (c) Between 480 and 479 BC
4. (d) Between 415 and 413 BC
5. (c) In the 16th century
6. (a) King Philip II
7. (b) Between 1271 and 1279
8. (c) Alexander the Great, after his death in 323 BC
9. (d) Between 750 and 550 BC
10. (a) 1453

Quiz No 16

1. When did the Peloponnesian War take place?
a. Between 131 and 104 BC

b.   Between 231 and 204 BC

c.   Between 531 and 504 BC

d.   Between 431 and 404 BC

2.   When was the first Greek colonization established in the Mediterranean world?

    a.   750 BC

    b.   150 BC

    c.   350 BC

    d.   550 BC

3.   When did the Mongol invasion in the north of China take place, when much of the land went out of cultivation, many cities and industries perished, and countless people died or became slaves?

    a.   Between 1411 and 1434

    b.   Between 1011 and 1034

    c.   Between 1211 and 1234

    d.   Between 1111 and 1134

4.   Where can you visit the Angkor wat temples, dating back from 9th to 13th centuries?

    a.   Cambodia

    b.   Sri Lanka

    c.   India

    d.   Thailand

5.   A charismatic leader of the Mongols, Temujin (1167-1227) gained recognition as supreme ruler and in 1206 took the title Genghis Khan. What was the meaning of the title Genghis Khan?

    a.   Prince of all that lies between the oceans

    b.   Greatest leader

    c.   Most powerful king

    d.   Son of God

6. Before 1,000 BC, which of the following was a prominent religious belief across Eurasia?

    a.   Zoroastrianism

    b.   Polytheism

    c.   Judaism

    d.   Hinduism

7. Which century brought to an end the rise and consolidation of national monarchies in western Europe?

    a.   12th century

    b.   18th century

    c.   14th century

    d.   16th century

8. In which of the following continents were all the significant world religions originated?

    a.   Antarctica

    b.   Australia

    c.   Asia

    d.   Africa

9. Owing to rebellion against Roman rule, when was a Jewish temple destroyed in Jerusalem?

    a.   AD 70

    b.   AD 470

    c.   AD 270

    d.   AD 170

10. Most religions of the world thrived along the trade routes and flourished under strong governments that established peace?

    a.   True

    b.   False

c.   None of the above

Answers Quiz 16

1. (d) Between 431 and 404 BC
2. (a) 750 BC
3. (c) Between 1211 and 1234
4. (a) Cambodia
5. (a) Prince of all that lies between the oceans
6. (b) Polytheism
7. (c) 14th century
8. (c) Asia
9. (a) AD 70
10. (a) True

Quiz No 17

1. Cyrus and Darius the Great were distinguished rulers of which of the following empires?
    a.   Persian
    b.   Ottoman
    c.   Mughal
    d.   Roman

2. Which city founded in the 8th century served as the capital of the six Muslim dynasties?
    a.   Lahore
    b.   Kolkata
    c.   Delhi
    d.   Mumbai

3. Chou was one of the most distinguished rulers of which of the following empires?
   a. Spanish
   b. Persian
   c. Roman
   d. Chinese

4. When did Buddhism reach Sri Lanka?
   a. In the late 2nd century BC
   b. In the late 1rst century BC
   c. In the late 3rd century BC
   d. In the late 5th century BC

5. After defeating which of the following empires, the Roman Republic annexed Sicily in 241 BC, Spain 206 BC and North Africa in 146 BC?
   a. Hittite
   b. Carthage
   c. Achaemenid
   d. Akkadian

6. Which region is situated at one of the world's main cross-roads?
   a. Middle East
   b. Eurasia
   c. South-East Asia
   d. Central Africa

7. Harappan civilization was established in which of the following periods?
   a. Bronze Age
   b. Middle Ages
   c. Iron Age
   d. Ice Age

8. Where did the Inca empire flourish?
   a.   Mexico
   b.   Peru
   c.   Syria
   d.   Iraq

9. Which of these long remained the language of churchmen and scientists?
   a.   Tamil
   b.   Farsi
   c.   Arabic
   d.   Latin

10. On continent Europe, under whose leadership the Franks converted to Christianity and began to expand south and east?
   a.   Julius Caesar
   b.   Alexander the Great
   c.   Clovis
   d.   Charlemagne

Answers Quiz 17

1.   (a) Persian Empire
2.   (c) Delhi
3.   (d) Chinese
4.   (c) In the late 3rd century BC
5.   (b) Carthage
6.   (c) South-East Asia
7.   (a) Bronze Age
8.   (b) Peru
9.   (d) Latin

10. (c) Clovis (481-511)

Quiz No 18

1. Which of the following laws forms the basis of the most modern western legal system?
    a.   Roman law
    b.   Statuate
    c.   Corpus Habeas
    d.   Magna Carta

2. Between 968 and about 1170 who controlled much of the valley of Mexico from their capital at Tula?
    a.   Ottomans
    b.   Portuguese
    c.   Toltecs
    d.   Mongols

3. When did Parthians and Germans invade Italy?
    a.   AD 370
    b.   AD 270
    c.   AD 70
    d.   AD 170

4. In the 7th century AD, in the wake of the upheavals that destroyed the ancient world, who managed to dominate the plains of Asia from the Great Wall of China to the Black Sea?
    a.   A confederation of Toltec tribes
    b.   A confederation of Turkish tribes
    c.   A confederation of Aztec tribes
    d.   A confederation of Mongol tribes

5. When was the last western Roman emperor defeated and the Western Roman Empire collapsed?

  a.   AD 476
  b.   AD 676
  c.   AD 276
  d.   AD 76

6. Which of these was the first dynasty of China?

  a.   Shang
  b.   Sui
  c.   Tang
  d.   Song

7. Who was a Kurdish military hero, the 12th century sultan and nemesis of the crusaders, and his demise was at the age of 56 in 1193 AD?

  a.   Ali Ibn Talib
  b.   Umar Ibn Khattab
  c.   Sultan Muhammad Fateh
  d.   Sultan Saladin Ayubi

8. Which of the following Roman leaders established himself as Princeps (first citizen) and adopted the title of Augustus in 27 BC?

  a.   Octavian
  b.   Clovis
  c.   Julius Caesar
  d.   Alexander the Great

9. Which city founded in the 8th century served as the capital of all of Turkish or Afghans extraction, who sought to extend their rule into the Deccan between 1206 and 1526?

  a.   Lahore

b. Delhi

c. Kolkata

d. Agra

10. Followers of which of the following religions worship numerous gods?

a. Hinduism

b. Buddhism

c. Zoroastrianism

d. Judaism

Answers Quiz 18

1. (a) Roman law

2. (c) Toltecs

3. (d) AD 170

4. (b) A confederation of Turkish tribes

5. (a) AD 476

6. (a) Shang

7. (d) Sultan Saladin Ayubi (1137-1197)

8. (a) Octavian

9. (b) Delhi

10. (a) Hinduism

Quiz No 19

1. Which of the following periods was China politically fragmented?

a. Between AD 220 and 589

b. Between AD 420 and 789

c. Between AD 320 and 689

d. Between AD 120 and 489

2. By the 3rd century AD, which of the following empires was ruling on the whole Mediterranean world and much of Europe?

   a. Roman Empire

   b. Egyptian Empire

   c. Assyrian Empire

   d. Carthaginian Empire

3. When did the central authority in Japan collapse?

   a. 1030s

   b. 1530s

   c. 1430s

   d. 1330s

4. When did the Mongols make their destructive conquests against Kievan Russia?

   a. Between 1037 and 1040

   b. Between 1137 and 1140

   c. Between 1237 and 1240

   d. Between 1337 and 1340

5. Where was the first grooved pottery, which is so distinctive of the Stone Age era, made in ancient Britain?

   a. Avebury

   b. Stonehenge

   c. Orkney

   d. Silbury Hill

6. Discovery of the Maqar Civilization does show, when and where was the first domestication of horses taken place?

a. About 6,000 years ago in the Dingle Peninsula
b. About 9,000 years ago in the Arabian Peninsula
c. About 7,000 years ago in the Lizard Peninsula
d. About 8,000 years ago in the Cape Peninsula

7. When was the grandson of Babur, Akbar the Great, ruler in India?
  a. Between 1356 and 1405
  b. Between 1656 and 1705
  c. Between 1456 and 1505
  d. Between 1556 and 1605

8. Remains of *Homo Sapiens* from South-East Asia date to when?
  a. 40 BC
  b. 400 BC
  c. 40000 BC
  d. 4000 BC

9. Choose True or False: Transition from hunter-gatherer to farmer was relatively gradual?
  a. True
  b. False
  c. All of the above
  d. None of the above

10. Which of these were included in the Heptarchy, seven separate Anglo-Saxon kingdoms, which rose in England in the 7th century?
  a. Hampshire, Hertfordshire, Isle of Wight, Camelot, Kent, North Yorkshire, and Rutland
  b. Bedfordshire, Cornwall, Buckinghamshire, Cleveland, Kent, Bristol and Wessex

c. Northumbria, Mercia, East Anglia, Camelot, Kent, Sussex and Wessex

d. Devon, Cheshire, East Anglia, Shropshire, Dorset, Sussex and Lincolnshire

Answers Quiz 19

1. (a) Between AD 220 and 589
2. (a) Roman Empire
3. (d) 1330s
4. (c) Between 1237 and 1240
5. (c) Orkney, Scotland
6. (b) About 9,000 years ago in the Arabian Peninsula
7. (d) Between 1556 and 1605
8. (c) 40,000 BC
9. (a) True
10. (c) Northumbria, Mercia, East Anglia, Camelot, Kent, Sussex and Wessex

Quiz No 20

1. Who defeated a large Roman army outside Adrianople in AD 378?
   a. Cybergoths
   b. Mesogoths
   c. Visigoths
   d. Shoggoths

2. During the Iron Age, which of the following regions was part of Western Europe, where Celtic tribes' settlements were established?
   a. Maya
   b. Aztec
   c. Inca
   d. Gaul

3. When was the Terracotta Warriors site discovered in the Chinese city of Xian?
   a. 1994
   b. 1964
   c. 1974
   d. 1984

4. Which of the following nomadic tribes occupied northern Italy?
   a. Lombards
   b. Dhangars
   c. Chukchis
   d. Balochs

5. Under whose leadership the Mongol empire stretched from the Pacific Ocean to the Caspian Sea?
   a. Attila the Hun
   b. Genghis Khan
   c. Timur
   d. Nero

6. Which of these is a World Heritage Site?
   a. Ring of Brodgar
   b. Acropolis of Athens
   c. Ancient city of Aleppo
   d. All of the above

7. About 6,000 years ago, the dispersed villages of Neolithic peoples gave way to more complex societies. What are these complex societies known as?

    a. Visigoths

    b. Mongols

    c. Toltecs

    d. First civilizations

8. What does 'Islam' mean?

    a. Submission to the will of God

    b. Freedom from material world through purification of desires and elimination of personal identity

    c. One can liberate from sufferings of life through by cultivating wisdom, virtue and concentration

    d. Good deeds are required in the cosmic struggle against the evil spirits

9. When were the great cities of Eurasia, such as Rome and Chang-an, in serious decline?

    a. AD 800

    b. AD 400

    c. AD 600

    d. AD 200

10. What was the characteristic feature of all the first civilizations?

    a. City

    b. School

    c. Temple

    d. Tomb

Answers Quiz 20

1. (c) Visigoths, western alliances of nomadic groups
2. (d) Gaul
3. (c) 1974
4. (a) Lombards
5. (b) Genghis Khan (1167-1227)
6. (d) All of the above
7. (d) The first civilizations
8. (a) Submission to the will of God
9. (c) AD 600
10. (a) City

Quiz No 21

1. The nomadic tribes of the Franks, Visigoths and Ostrogoths adopted local adopted life in which countries?
    a. Franks in Hungary, Visigoths in Poland and Ostrogoths in Norway
    b. Franks in Italy, Visigoths in France and Ostrogoths in Spain
    c. Franks in France, Visigoths in Spain and Ostrogoths in Italy
    d. Franks in Switzerland, Visigoths in Britain and Ostrogoths in Germany

2. Except during the reign of which of the following rulers was the west always neglected in the Roman empire?
    a. Justinian
    b. Augustus

c. Hadrian

d. Trajan

3. When did the Mongol forces make unsuccessful amphibious expeditions against Japan?
   a. In 1474 and 1481
   b. In 1374 and 1381
   c. In 1174 and 1181
   d. In 1274 and 1281

4. When was the treaty of Verdun signed which created three kingdoms: one in east, one in the west and a middle kingdom in Europe?
   a. AD 1043
   b. AD 843
   c. AD 743
   d. AD 943

5. Traces of 'Java man' from South-East Asia date back to when?
   a. From middle Pliocene
   b. From middle Pleistocene
   c. From middle Holocene
   d. From middle Paleolithic

6. When was the last Roman emperor deposed in the west?
   a. AD 376
   b. AD 276
   c. AD 676
   d. AD 476

7. When did Hsien-pi invade north China?
   a. AD 41
   b. AD 641

c.   AD 441

d.   AD 241

8. For Jews which of these is the City of David, the place
where King David created the first Israelite capital?
a.   Nazareth
b.   Jerusalem
c.   Haifa
d.   Tel Aviv

9. When did the Hopewell chiefs of Ohio and Illinois
build complex burial mounds and established trade
contacts with Florida to the Rockies?
a.   Between 300 BC and AD 550
b.   Between 400 BC and AD 450
c.   Between AD 200 and AD 950
d.   Between 100 BC and AD 750

10. When did the Seljuk Turks crush the Byzantine forces
at Manzikert?
a.   1171
b.   971
c.   1071
d.   1371

Answers Quiz 21

1. (c) Franks in France, Visigoths in Spain and Ostrogoths
in Italy
2. (a) Justinian
3. (d) In 1274 and 1281
4. (b) AD 843
5. (b) From middle Pleistocene

6. (d) AD 476

7. (c) AD 441

8. (b) Jerusalem

9. (a) Between 300 BC and AD 550

10. (c) 1071

Quiz No 22

1. Which of these is a testament to a period of transition in England between paganism and Christianity?
   a. Protestantism
   b. Reformation
   c. Enlightenment
   d. Anglo-Saxon ship burial at Sutton Hoo

2. In the 8th century, which of these cities was founded in the Subcontinent by a Rajput chief?
   a. Varanasi
   b. Ayodhya
   c. Delhi
   d. Patna

3. Who brought the first seed grain of wheat and barley to Britain?
   a. Neolithic farmers
   b. Anglo-Saxons
   c. Romans
   d. Vikings

4. Intensity of which conflict stemmed from the religious division within Islam between Sunnite and Shi'ite,

which excited the same passion at the split between
Protestant and Catholic Christians at the same time?
- a.   Wahhabism in Saudi Arabia
- b.   Sunnite Ottomans and Shi'ite Persia
- c.   Crusades
- d.   Battles of Badr, Uhad and Khandaq

5.   Which of the following diseases was particularly
virulent in Europe, and few who caught it ever
recovered?
- a.   Smallpox
- b.   Malaria
- c.   Black Death
- d.   Poliomyelitis

6.   By the 18th century, how many European states
maintained almost 50 fortified trading posts on the west
coast, from Arguin to Lagos?
- a.   3
- b.   5
- c.   7
- d.   9

7.   Where has the discovery of Maqar Civilization been
made which shows the domestication of horses took
place 9,000 years ago?
- a.   Mongolia
- b.   Saudi Arabia
- c.   Kenya
- d.   Turkey

8.   In 1206, the foundation of which empire was laid down
in India that stretched over 320 years until 1526?
- a.   Mughal Empire
- b.   Mongol Empire

c.   Delhi Sultanate

d.   British Empire

9.   When did Portuguese establish trading posts at Arguin?

a.   1482

b.   1582

c.   1382

d.   1782

10. What was the introduction of farming in human history?

a.   When the people learned about seasons

b.   When the people got bored of hunting and gathering

c.   When the people learned how the combination of sunlight, water and earth can help produce crops, plants and fruits

d.   When the people learned how to produce rather than acquire their food

Answers Quiz 22

1.   (d) Anglo-Saxon ship burial at Sutton Hoo

2.   (c) Delhi

3.   (a) Neolithic farmers

4.   (b) Sunnite Ottomans and Shi'ite Persia, initiated when Sunnite Ottomans under Salim I invaded Persia in 1514 and captured Tabriz

5.   (c) Black Death which mainly spread by infected fleas carried by rats

6.   (d) 9

7.   (b) Saudi Arabia

8.   (c) Delhi Sultanate

9. (a) 1482

10. (d) When the people learned how to produce rather than acquire their food

Quiz No 23

1. When did the Roman Empire collapse?
    a.   AD 654
    b.   AD 354
    c.   AD 454
    d.   AD 554

2. One of the greatest manifestations of the "creative psyche" in the whole of Egyptian history was the attempt (unsuccessful in the end) of which of the following pharaohs to introduce monotheism in the 14th century B.C.?
    a.   Ramses II
    b.   Khufu
    c.   Pharaoh Akhenaten
    d.   Djoser

3. Under the leadership of Attila, when did Romans defeat the Huns at Chalons?
    a.   AD 151
    b.   AD 251
    c.   AD 651
    d.   AD 451

4. During which of the following centuries did the alliance of nomadic tribes known as the Huns, swept south-westwards through Asia, initiating a chain reaction

among the Germanic people along the Black Sea and
the Danube?
- a. In the 2nd and 3rd centuries
- b. In the 4th and 5th centuries
- c. In the 5th and 6th centuries
- d. In the 1rst and 2nd centuries

5. When did the Mongol empire establish in Eurasia?
- a. After 1206
- b. After 1006
- c. After 1606
- d. After 1406

6. Who is a famous Egyptologist and a pioneer of
systematic methodology in archaeology and artefacts?
- a. Flinders Petrie
- b. Robert Braitwood
- c. Carl Blegen
- d. W. F. Albright

7. When was a series of pioneering voyages of exploration
from Europe taken place which laid the foundation for
overseas expansion?
- a. In the second half of the 11th century
- b. In the second half of the 17th century
- c. In the second half of the 16th century
- d. In the second half of the 15th century

8. Which of the following religions embarked on as a
Jewish splinter movement in Roman Palestine?
- a. Islam
- b. Christianity
- c. Hinduism
- d. Buddhism

9. Under which dynasty was, for the first time a unified China emerged by 221 BC?
    a. Ch'in
    b. Xia
    c. Shang
    d. Han

10. Anglo-Saxon ship burial at Sutton Hoo, the grave excavated in Suffolk, in England dates back to when?
    a. AD 450
    b. AD 350
    c. AD 650
    d. AD 550

Answers Quiz 23

1. (c) AD 454
2. (c) Pharaoh Akhenaten (or Ikhnaton)
3. (d) AD 451
4. (b) In the 4th and 5th centuries
5. (a) After 1206
6. (a) Sir Flinders Petrie
7. (d) In the second half of the 15th century
8. (b) Christianity
9. (a) Ch'in dynasty under the leadership of Shih Huang-ti (first emperor)
10. (c) AD 650

Quiz No 24

1. Under Casimir III (1339-70) which region made significant development?
    a. Hungary
    b. Poland
    c. Czech Republic
    d. Greece

2. Who is the founder of the Christianity, which was initiated as a Jewish splinter movement in Roman Palestine?
    a. Jesus of Nazareth
    b. Muhammad Ibn Abdullah
    c. Siddhartha Gautama
    d. Abraham

3. Which of these was the fourth ecumenical council that tried to impose orthodoxy on the Christian world?
    a. Council of Ephesus
    b. Council of Nicaea
    c. Council of Chalcedon
    d. Council of Constantinople

4. Missionaries sent by the Nestorians of Persia in the 7th century spread Christianity in which of the following regions?
    a. Africa
    b. Eurasia
    c. Arabia
    d. China

5. When did the Moorish kingdom of Granada collapse?
    a. 1392
    b. 1692
    c. 1592
    d. 1492

6. After the barbarian invasions of the 4th and 5th centuries, which of the following dynasties reunified China?

    a.   Sui dynasty
    b.   Zhou dynasty
    c.   Qin dynasty
    d.   Song dynasty

7. How can you define the start of the Neolithic or New Stone Age?

    a.   Change from a farming to a industrial way of life
    b.   Change from a hunter-gatherer to a farming way of life
    c.   Change from a rural to a city way of life
    d.   Change from a nomadic to a settled way of life

8. According to a European visitor, who was 'the most powerful man since Adam'?

    a.   Salahuddin Ayubi
    b.   Hammurabi
    c.   Kublai Khan
    d.   Adolf Hitler

9. Until when was the racial segregation prevalent all over the world?

    a.   The 1290s
    b.   The 1690s
    c.   The 1490s
    d.   The 1590s

10. When was the fourth ecumenical council, the council of Chalcedon, held?

    a.   AD 751

b.   AD 651
c.   AD 351
d.   AD 451

Answers Quiz 24

1. (b) Poland
2. (a) Jesus of Nazareth
3. (c) Council of Chalcedon
4. (c) (d) Arabia and China
5. (d) 1492
6. (a) Sui dynasty
7. (b) Change from a hunter-gatherer to a farming way of life
8. (c) Kublai Khan
9. (c) The 1490s
10. (d) AD 451

Quiz No 25

1. From the reign of which of the following rulers did the Roman empire become an eastern Greek speaking state known as Byzantium?
    a.   Heraclius
    b.   Hadrian
    c.   Trajan
    d.   Marcus Aurelius

2. Which of the following monuments can you visit near Amesbury, Wiltshire?

    a. Skara Brae

    b. Angkor

    c. Stonehenge

    d. Machu Picchu

3. When were the followers of Prophet Muhammad (PBUH) forced to migrate Medina to avoid to the hostility of the merchants of Mecca?

    a. AD 722

    b. AD 622

    c. AD 822

    d. AD 522

4. What are these: a 5,000-year-old village of Skara Brae; the giant chambered grave of Maeshowe; a Stone Age mausoleum whose internal walls were later carved with runes by Vikings; and the Stones of Stenness and the Ring of Brodgar and the Ness of Brodgar?

    a. Some of the finest Medieval monuments in the world

    b. Some of the finest Paleolithic monuments in the world

    c. Some of the finest Chalcolithic monuments in the world

    d. Some of the finest Neolithic monuments in the world

5. During which of the following centuries did the Seljuk Turks emerge?

    a. In the 11th century

    b. In the 13th century

    c. In the 12th century

    d. In the 10th century

6. When did Heraclius defeat Persians at Nineveh?

a. AD 828
b. AD 628
c. AD 528
d. AD 728

7. When did the schism develop between Orthodox and Catholic churches?
   a. 1354
   b. 1254
   c. 1054
   d. 1154

8. Which of these is considered as the most significant development in world history between the collapse of the Roman Empire and the European invasion of the Americas?
   a. The Battle of Hastings in 1066
   b. Rise and expansion of Islam
   c. The sealing of Magna Carta in 1215
   d. Pandemic of the Black Death

9. Neolithic people - the first farmers - gave way to more complex societies. What are these known as?
   a. First civilizations
   b. Aegean civilization
   c. Harappan civilization
   d. Bronze Age collapse

10. When was the foundation of Dominican and Franciscan orders laid down?
   a. 1316
   b. 1016
   c. 1116
   d. 1216

Answers Quiz 25

1. (a) Heraclius (AD 610-641)
2. (c) Stonehenge
3. (b) AD 622
4. (d) Some of the finest Neolithic monuments in the world
5. (a) In the 11th century
6. (b) AD 628
7. (c) 1054
8. (b) The rise and expansion of Islam
9. (a) The First civilizations
10. (d) 1216

Quiz No 26

1. In Islam World, which of the following dynasties was established after the Umayyad dynasty?
   a. Mughal empire
   b. Abbasid caliphate
   c. Mamluks
   d. Ottoman empire

2. Where can you visit the great mosque of Cordoba?
   a. Palestine
   b. Iran
   c. Spain
   d. Turkey

3. When did the Spaniards arrive on the American mainland?

a. Early 17th century
b. Early 14th century
c. Early 15th century
d. Early 16th century

4. Where were the first henges - stone rings with ditches around them, which is so distinctive of the Stone Age era, erected in ancient Britain?
    a. Orkney, Scotland
    b. Wiltshire, England
    c. Gwent, Wales
    d. Londonderry, Northern Ireland

5. What is the arrival of farming as a major and rapid change rather than a gradual transition known as?
    a. Neolithic revolution
    b. Haitian revolution
    c. Industrial revolution
    d. Spring revolution

6. Which century brought to an end the agricultural boom that had prevailed since 1150 in western Europe?
    a. 16th century
    b. 12th century
    c. 14th century
    d. 18th century

7. How long did it take for farming to spread across all parts of the British Isles?
    a. About 1,000 years
    b. About 3,000 years
    c. About 4,000 years
    d. About 2,000 years

8. When was the famous Stonehenge monument seemed to have developed out of the causewayed enclosure which incorporated lunar and solar alignments?
   a. Around 3000 BC
   b. Around 4000 BC
   c. Around 2000 BC
   d. Around 5000 BC

9. Which of the following dynasties established a uniform administrative organisation of states, in which officials were recruited through an examination?
   a. Shang
   b. Tang
   c. Han
   d. Zhou

10. When did Hindu-Buddhist influences reach South-East Asia?
    a. Around 6th or 7th century
    b. Around 4th or 5th century
    c. Around 2nd or 3rd century
    d. Around 5ft or 6th century

Answers Quiz 26

1. (b) Abbasid caliphate
2. (c) Spain
3. (d) Early 16th century
4. (a) Orkney, Scotland
5. (a) Neolithic revolution
6. (c) 14th century
7. (d) About 2,000 years
8. (a) Around 3000 BC

9. (b) Tang dynasty between AD 618 and 907

10. (c) Around 2nd or 3rd century

Quiz No 27

1. Pippin and his son Charles Martel founded which dynasty in Europe?
   a. Carolingian
   b. Rurik
   c. Medici
   d. Habsburg

2. When did the Buddhist images and votive tablets, along with Sanskrit inscriptions appear in South-East Asia?
   a. By the 3rd century AD
   b. By the 4th century AD
   c. By the 5th century AD
   d. By the 6th century AD

3. When was Clovis the ruler during whose reign Frankish conversion to Christianity took place?
   a. Between 581 and 611
   b. Between 281 and 311
   c. Between 381 and 411
   d. Between 481 and 511

4. When did one of the rebel leaders, Chu Yuan-chang, gradually overcame his rivals and established a new dynasty, the Ming, in China?
   a. 1568
   b. 1368
   c. 1468

d. 1268

5. Whose coronation as emperor of the west did take place in Rome?
    a. Charlemagne
    b. Constantine the Great
    c. Henry VIII
    d. Augustus

6. When did Babur defeat the last of the Sultans of Delhi at Panipat in Indian Subcontinent?
    a. 1626
    b. 1226
    c. 1426
    d. 1526

7. Which were three separate groups of invaders in the 9th century who shattered the relative stability achieved by Charlemagne in western Europe and by Offa of Mercia in England?
    a. Saracens, Magyars, Chechens
    b. Saracens, Magyars, Vikings
    c. Red Brigade, Magyars, Vikings
    d. Saracens, Catalans, Vikings

8. Success of which of these in Europe was largely achieved not through superior organization or tactical skill, but depended on their greater mobility?
    a. Chechens
    b. Magyars
    c. Vikings
    d. Saracens

9. Where can you visit the Borobudur and Prambanan temples, dating back from the 8th to 10th centuries?

a. Sri Lanka
b. India
c. Cambodia
d. Java

10. Ness of Brodgar in Orkney is comparable to which of the following sites in England?
    a. Chichester cross
    b. Stonehenge
    c. Cerne giant
    d. Yarborough monument

Answers Quiz 27

1. (a) Carolingian
2. (c) By the 5th century AD
3. (d) Between 481 and 511
4. (b) 1368
5. (a) Charles the Great or Charlemagne
6. (d) 1526
7. (b) Saracens, Magyars of Hungary, and Vikings from Scandinavia
8. (c) Vikings
9. (d) Central Java
10. (b) Stonehenge, Wiltshire

Quiz No 28

1. What were the three factors that shaped the early history of Russia?

a. Eastward movement of Slav settlers
b. Impact of the Vikings from the north
c. Division of the region into forests and treeless steppe
d. All of the above

2. Which of the following cities founded in the 8th century remained the focus of north Indian politics?
   a. Delhi
   b. Chennai
   c. Mumbai
   d. Kolkata

3. How many Africans were shipped abroad by Europeans between 1450 and 1870, almost 90 percent went to South America and the Caribbean, most of them during the 18th century?
   a. About 14 million
   b. About 8 million
   c. About 12 million
   d. About 10 million

4. Which is the most important Neolithic monument excavated recently on Orkney archipelago?
   a. Avebury
   b. Ness of Brodgar
   c. Callanish Stones
   d. Mitchell's Fold

5. Which continent is known as the 'dark continent'?
   a. Asia
   b. South America
   c. Africa
   d. Antarctica

6. Which of these were the main centres of Indus valley civilization?
- a. Harappa
- b. Fatehpur Sikri
- c. Kandy
- d. Mohenjo-Daro

7. When did the power of Asante arise?
- a. 1700
- b. 1500
- c. 1600
- d. 1800

8. In the first half of the 13th century, who made a sudden and devastating irruption into world history?
- a. Vikings
- b. Mongols
- c. Spaniards
- d. Saracens

9. When did the people of Neolithic, the first farmers in Britain, arrive on Orkney?
- a. About 3,000 years ago
- b. About 4,000 years ago
- c. About 5,000 years ago
- d. About 6,000 years ago

10. In Islamic World, which of the following cities was the capital of the Caliphs?
- a. Damascus
- b. Istanbul
- c. Baghdad
- d. Cairo

Answers Quiz 28

1. (d) All of the above
2. (a) Delhi
3. (c) About 12 million
4. (b) Ness of Brodgar
5. (c) Africa
6. (a) (d) Harappa in Punjab and Mohenjo-Daro in Sindh
7. (a) 1700
8. (b) Mongols
9. (d) About 6,000 years ago
10. (c) Baghdad

Quiz No 29

1. When did the Mongols suffer a defeat at Ain Jalut at the hands of Mamluks of Egypt and withdrew to Persia?
   a. 3 September 1360
   b. 3 September 1260
   c. 3 September 1460
   d. 3 September 1060

2. Through which route silver and gold from Europe and the Near East reached China while Chinese silks and porcelain circulated in Europe?
   a. Silk Road
   b. Great Ocean Road
   c. Orchard Road
   d. Abbey Road

3. Which city founded in the 8th century remained the centre of Muslim culture from the 13th to the 19th century?
   a. Kolkata
   b. Agra
   c. Lahore
   d. Delhi

4. Which of these created fortified bases around the Indian Ocean in the early 16th century?
   a. Dutch
   b. Portuguese
   c. English
   d. French

5. Where can you visit the archaeological site Pagan, dating back from the 11th to 13th centuries?
   a. Sri Lanka
   b. Cambodia
   c. Burma
   d. Thai Land

6. When did the Spaniards capture the Muslim fort at Manila?
   a. 1871
   b. 1471
   c. 1571
   d. 1671

7. When did *Homo Sapiens* spread throughout South-East Asia?
   a. 600 BC
   b. 600,000 BC
   c. 6,000 BC
   d. 60,000 BC

8. Under Luis the Great (1342-82) which region made profound progress?
- a. Hungary
- b. Britain
- c. North America
- d. South America

9. Who established a new dynasty, the Ming, in China in 1368?
- a. Genghis Khan
- b. Chu Yuan-chang
- c. Kublai Khan
- d. Qin Shi Huang

10. When did Portuguese traders arrive in Japan?
- a. 1543
- b. 1343
- c. 1643
- d. 1443

Answers Quiz 29

1. (b) 3 September 1260
2. (a) Silk Road
3. (d) Delhi
4. (b) Portuguese
5. (c) Burma/Myanmar
6. (c) 1571
7. (d) 60,000 BC
8. (a) Hungary
9. (b) One of the rebel leaders, Chu Yuan-chang
10. (a) 1543

Quiz No 30

1. When did the Tokugawa Ieyasu become the first Tokugawa shogun in Japan?
- a. 1703
- b. 1403
- c. 1503
- d. 1603

2. Which of the following monuments of ancient Britain incorporate lunar and solar alignments?
- a. Stonehenge
- b. Avebury
- c. Ring of Brodgar
- d. All of the above

3. The overthrow of which dynasty by the Mongols in 1256-60 left the Muslim world in disarray for half a century?
- a. Seljuk Empire
- b. Mughal Empire
- c. Abbasid Caliphate
- d. Umayyad Caliphate

4. Where can you visit some of the finest Neolithic monuments in the world such as the 5,000-year-old village of Skara Brae, the giant chambered grave of Maeshowe, a Stone Age mausoleum whose internal walls were later carved with runes by Vikings, and the Stones of Stenness and the Ring of Brodgar and the Ness of Brodgar?

a. Avebury
b. Orkney
c. Wiltshire
d. Devonshire

5. When did the Mayan civilization flourish?
   a. Before Spain conquered the region
   b. Before Aztecs conquered the region
   c. Before Incas conquered the region
   d. Before Portuguese conquered the region

6. In Britain, what is the preceding period of the last, post-glacial hunter-gatherer societies known as?
   a. Cretaceous
   b. Mesolithic
   c. Triassic
   d. Cenozoic

7. Which of these was the Chinese Muslim admiral who commanded a succession of Chinese voyages in the early 15th century and secured tribute and extended recognition of the new Ming dynasty?
   a. Cheng Ho
   b. Genghis Khan
   c. Kublai Khan
   d. Taizu

8. Which of the following was the common African ancestor of *Homo erectus* and *Homo heidelbergensis*?
   a. Homo ergaster
   b. Homo sapiens
   c. Homo habilis
   d. Homo neanderthalensis

9. When did Aztecs arrive at Tenochtitlan?

a. 1225
b. 1525
c. 1325
d. 1425

10. When did a Turkish leader named Osman found a state which became the core of the future Ottoman empire?
a. 1400
b. 1300
c. 1200
d. 1000

Answers Quiz 30

1. (d) 1603
2. (d) Henge monuments like Stonehenge, Avebury, Ring of Brodgar
3. (c) Abbasid Caliphate
4. (b) Orkney archipelago, Scotland
5. (a) Before Spain conquered the region
6. (b) Mesolithic or Middle Stone Age
7. (a) Cheng Ho/Zheng He
8. (a) Homo ergaster
9. (c) 1325
10. (b) 1300

Quiz No 31

1. Since the 1490s, which of these is the central feature of world history?

a. Expansion of Asia and the spread of Asian civilization throughout the globe
b. Expansion of Europe and the spread of European civilization throughout the globe
c. Expansion of South America and the spread of South American civilization throughout the globe
d. Expansion of Latin America and the spread of Latin American civilization throughout the globe

2. Between 3 and 4 million years ago, whose skeletal and fossilized footprints does indicate a serviceable if not fully bipedal gait, hands still partly adapted for specialized tree climbing and a brain approximately one-third the size of ours?
   a. Australopithecus afarensis
   b. Homo sapiens
   c. Homo ergaster
   d. Homo neanderthalensis

3. In America which empire collapsed suddenly in 1521?
   a. Olmec
   b. Nasca
   c. Aztec
   d. Inca

4. After Greece including the island of Euboea, where were the first Phoenician exploration and settlements established after 750 BC?
   a. Britain
   b. Italy
   c. France
   d. Sicily

5. When did Shah Ismail found the Safavid dynasty in Persia?

    a.   1200

    b.   1600

    c.   1400

    d.   1500

6. When were the first African slaves shipped to the Americas?

    a.   1510

    b.   1710

    c.   1410

    d.   1610

7. When were the potatoes introduced to Europe from South America?

    a.   1765

    b.   1165

    c.   1565

    d.   1365

8. What is the introduction of farming - when people learned how to produce rather than acquire their food - widely regarded as?

    a.   One of the smallest changes in human history

    b.   One of the biggest changes in human history

    c.   One of the big changes in human history

    d.   One of the small changes in human history

9. Which of the following periods witnessed the appearance of the first large communal tombs, known as long barrows, or mounds, and the earliest ceremonial monuments, known as causewayed enclosures?

    a.   Middle Neolithic

    b.   Bronze Age

c. Chalcolithic

d. Mesolithic

10. Which period did see the start of the so-called 'Celtic' way of life?

a. Iron age

b. Middle Ages

c. Late Bronze Age

d. Stone Age

Answers Quiz 31

1. (b) Expansion of Europe and the spread of European civilization throughout the globe
2. (a) Australopithecus afarensis
3. (c) Aztec
4. (b) (d) Italy and Sicily
5. (d) 1500
6. (a) 1510
7. (c) 1565
8. (b) One of the biggest changes in human history
9. (a) Middle Neolithic
10. (c) Late Bronze Age (1250 BC - 800 BC)

Quiz No 32

1. Which of the following varieties of pepper was the most valuable that was native to India and hard to transplant in the 16th century?

a. Peppercorn

    b.   Banana pepper
    c.   Cherry pepper
    d.   Poblano pepper

2.   Before which of the following years were civilizations
      essentially land centred and contacts by sea relatively
      unimportant?
      a.   1300
      b.   1600
      c.   1400
      d.   1500

3.   When did Europe inaugurate the process of
      transformation throughout the world which dethroned
      agricultural society as it had existed for thousands of
      years, replacing it with an urban, industrialized,
      technocratic society?
      a.   Between 1615 and 1714
      b.   Between 1915 and 2014
      c.   Between 1715 and 1814
      d.   Between 1815 and 1914

4.   In which crusade Sultan Saladin Ayubi (1137-1197)
      fought long and hard and in a very committed manner
      and died with a mysterious ailment possibly Typhoid?
      a.   Third
      b.   Second
      c.   Fourth
      d.   Fifth

5.   What is the Late Bronze Age?
      a.   1150 BC - 700 BC
      b.   1250 BC - 800 BC
      c.   1050 BC - 600 BC
      d.   1350 BC - 900 BC

6. By annexing the Sung dynasty, which of the following invaders captured all of China and for the first time all of China came under foreign rule?

    a.   Kublai Khan

    b.   Xiang Yo

    c.   Liu Bang

    d.   Han Xin

7. The whole world used to be joined in one supercontinent called Pangaea. Why did this supercontinent break up into different parts, eventually, creating the continents and countries we recognized today?

    a.   Volcanic eruption

    b.   Tectonic plates moving around

    c.   Meteorite strike

    d.   Great flood

8. Which of the following places is the heartland of the Neolith North?

    a.   Stonehenge

    b.   Maiden castle

    c.   Ness of Brodgar

    d.   Avebury

9. When was there a fundamental shift in burial practice away from barrow burial, towards cremation in large open cemeteries where ashes were placed in specially prepared pottery urns?

    a.   Iron Age

    b.   Late Bronze Age

    c.   Early Bronze Age

    d.   Middle Bronze Age

10. How old are the earliest known hominine fossils which come from the Afar region of Ethiopia?
    a.   1.5 million years
    b.   4.5 million years
    c.   3.5 million years
    d.   2.5 million years

Answers Quiz 32

1. (a) Piper nigrum commonly known as peppercorn
2. (d) 1500
3. (d) Between 1815 and 1914
4. (a) Third
5. (b) 1250 BC - 800 BC
6. (a) Kublai Khan in 1270s
7. (b) Tectonic plates moving around
8. (c) Ness of Brodgar, Orkney
9. (d) Middle Bronze Age (1500-1250 BC)
10. (b) 4.5 million years

Quiz No 33

1. Who were the first farmers in Britain?
    a.   People of Mesolithic
    b.   People of Chalcolithic
    c.   People of Paleolithic
    d.   People of Neolithic

2. Excavations on one of the first great civilizations, the Indus valley civilization, go back no further than which of the following years?
   a. 1955
   b. 1925
   c. 1945
   d. 1935

3. When did the dispersed villages of Neolithic peoples give way to more complex societies?
   a. About 6,000 years ago
   b. About 2,000 years ago
   c. About 4,000 years ago
   d. About 1,000 years ago

4. Which of the following first great civilizations had long histories, stretching more than 2,000 years before Alexander the Great forcibly brought them into the Greek orbit?
   a. Egypt
   b. Maya
   c. Inca
   d. Mesopotamia

5. Which of the following species is the probable ancestor both of the Australopithecus ('southern apes') and of our genus Homo ('man')?
   a. Paranthropus aethiopicus
   b. Australopithecus afarensis
   c. Ardipithecus ramidus
   d. Homo rhodesiensis

6. How long ago were the western Pacific islands colonized?
   a. By 31,000 years

b. By 35,000 years

c. By 37,000 years

d. By 33,000 years

7. A million years ago, who had migrated into North Africa and the Near East, reaching northern Europe about 500,000 years ago?

    a. Australopithecus afarensis

    b. Homo naledi

    c. Homo heidelbergensis

    d. Homo rhodesiensis

8. Until the 1490s, which of these remained concentrated in sub-Saharan Africa and a few Pacific islands?

    a. Negroids

    b. Mongoloids

    c. Caucasoids

    d. Australoids

9. When did Selim I from Ottoman empire defeat the new Safavid rulers of Persia and conquer the Mamluks?

    a. Between 1510 and 1518

    b. Between 1512 and 1520

    c. Between 1508 and 1516

    d. Between 1514 and 1522

10. The earliest wheat and barley were grown in which of the following parts of the globe?

    a. South-West Asia

    b. Northern Asia

    c. Western Asia

    d. Eastern Asia

Answers Quiz 33

1. (d) People of Neolithic - a new Stone Age
2. (c) 1945
3. (a) About 6,000 years ago
4. (a) (d) Egypt and Mesopotamia
5. (b) Australopithecus afarensis
6. (d) By 33,000 years
7. (c) Homo heidelbergensis
8. (a) Negroids
9. (b) Between 1512 and 1520
10. (a) South-West Asia

Quiz No 34

1. What are the Stones of Stenness and the Ring of Brodgar?
   a. Neolithic monuments found in Devonshire
   b. Neolithic monuments found in Kent
   c. Neolithic monuments found in Orkney
   d. Neolithic monuments found in Wiltshire

2. In AD 1,500, the world population was 350 million. How many were the hunters and gatherers?
   a. 50 percent
   b. 5.0 percent
   c. 10 percent
   d. 1.0 percent

3. After the migration of the earliest modern-looking human northward from Africa around 100,000 years

ago, when did modern human populations and settlements begin to grow again after a period of stagnation?

   a.   About 1000 years ago
   b.   About 10,000 years ago
   c.   About 50,000 years ago
   d.   About 5000 years ago

4. Which of these accounted for over 70 percent by volume of the world spice trade in the 16th century?

   a.   Pepper
   b.   Cumin
   c.   Cardamom
   d.   Clove

5. When were Neolithic monuments in Orkney given World Heritage status by UNESCO?

   a.   1999
   b.   1980
   c.   1989
   d.   1990

6. How old are the earliest modern-looking human (*Homo sapiens*) skulls yet found?

   a.   About 100,000 years
   b.   About 130,000 years
   c.   About 110,000 years
   d.   About 120,000 years

7. When did Portuguese establish trading posts in east Africa?

   a.   1605
   b.   1305
   c.   1405
   d.   1505

8. What were the ancestors of modern wheat and barley?
- a. Small-seeded weeds
- b. Large-seeded weeds
- c. Large-seeded grasses
- d. Small-seeded grasses

9. How old is one of the Seven Wonders of the Ancient World, the Great Pyramid of Giza?
- a. 6,500-years-old
- b. 2,500-years-old
- c. 3,500-years-old
- d. 4,500-years-old

10. Which powerful king from Babylon established his hegemony over the whole of southern Mesopotamia?
- a. Hammurabi
- b. Nerriglisser
- c. Abi-Eshuh
- d. Ammi-Ditana

Answers Quiz 34

1. (c) Neolithic monuments of two huge neighbouring circles of standing stones found in Orkney
2. (d) 1.0 percent
3. (c) About 50,000 years ago
4. (a) Pepper
5. (a) 1999
6. (b) About 130,000 years
7. (d) 1505
8. (c) Large-seeded grasses
9. (d) 4,500-years-old

10. (a) Hammurabi (1728-1686 BC)

Quiz No 35

1. What does define the change from a hunter-gatherer to a farming way of life?
    a. Start of Neolithic Age
    b. Start of Middle Age
    c. Start of Bronze Age
    d. Start of Iron Age

2. What led allowing hominines to remember, to manipulate, to support and to organize others in more complex ways?
    a. Homo's brains grew hardened
    b. Homo's brains grew flattened
    c. Homo's brains grew smaller
    d. Homo's brains grew larger

3. Which of the following peoples' traditional lifestyles do face the threat of extinction?
    a. Surviving representatives of Bronze Age
    b. Surviving representatives of Iron Age
    c. Surviving representatives of hunters and gatherers
    d. Surviving representatives of Middle Ages

4. What is the date of the earliest semi-permanent village in West Asia?
    a. 100 BC
    b. 10,000 BC
    c. 10 BC

       d.   1000 BC

5. Choose True or False: Development in Old and New Worlds (the Americas) adopted the identical path like the beginning of farming, the emergence of cities and empires and invention of writing?
- a. True
- b. False
- c. All of the above
- d. None of the above

6. Which of these is the centerpiece of the 5th-century Greek building campaign?
- a. Jacobethan
- b. Parthenon
- c. Renaissance
- d. Gothic

7. The terms such as Princeps (first citizen) and Dominus (absolute ruler) were adopted by the emperors of which of the following empires?
- a. Abbasid Caliphate
- b. Roman Republic
- c. Mongol Dynasty
- d. British Empire

8. Until the 1490s, which of these remained concentrated in Australia?
- a. Negroids
- b. Mongoloids
- c. Caucasoids
- d. Australoids

9. All the different gods of religion Hinduism, emphasise which of the following?

a. Love is religion
b. Banish of worldly possessions
c. Right way to live
d. Faith over fear

10. Under whose reign the Ottoman empire extended over one million square miles, with some 14 million inhabitants?
   a. Ertugrul
   b. Selim
   c. Murad
   d. Suleiman

Answers Quiz 35

1. (a) Start of Neolithic or New Stone Age
2. (d) Homo's brains grew larger
3. (c) Surviving representatives of hunters and gatherers
4. (b) 10,000 BC
5. (d) True
6. (b) Parthenon
7. (b) Roman Republic
8. (d) Australoids
9. (c) Right way to live
10. (c) Suleiman the Magnificent (1520-66)

Quiz No 36

1. Where are the Neolithic houses far more commonly found than in England and Wales?

a. Scotland
b. Ireland
c. All of the above
d. None of the above

2. For many thousands of years, with whom *Homo sapiens* shared the world in East Asia, and in Europe and West Asia?
   a. Homo erectus
   b. Ardipithecus
   c. Oreopithecus
   d. Neanderthals

3. Who were the 'Sea Peoples' that overran all the major powers of the Eastern Mediterranean and a 'Dark Age' was started off around 1,200 BC?
   a. Mongol
   b. Marauders
   c. Vikings
   d. Ottomans

4. What was the period of the III Ur empire, which was one of the early empires of Mesopotamia?
   a. Between 4,047 and 3,940 BC
   b. Between 3,047 and 2,940 BC
   c. Between 1,047 and 940 BC
   d. Between 2,047 and 1,940 BC

5. When did the Teotihuacan civilization emerge in Mesoamerica?
   a. Around AD 500
   b. Around AD 10
   c. Around AD 100
   d. Around AD 1000

6. When were the first cereals cultivated in Africa?
   a.   By 6,000 BC
   b.   By 7,000 BC
   c.   By 4,000 BC
   d.   By 5,000 BC

7. Which of these were the complex urban societies of Indus civilization established in the 3rd millennium?
   a.   Machu Picchu
   b.   Harappa
   c.   Mohenjo-Daro
   d.   Mesopotamia

8. When did Chandragupta Maurya seize the province of Trans-Indus from the successors of Alexander the Great?
   a.   405 BC
   b.   105 BC
   c.   205 BC
   d.   305 BC

9. When was the first Spanish settlement in the New World established?
   a.   1593
   b.   1293
   c.   1493
   d.   1393

10. Around 1,600 BC, who conquered the Crete and emerged as a prime military and economic power in the Aegean?
   a.   Mycenaeans
   b.   Mongols
   c.   Marauders
   d.   Vikings

Answers Quiz 36

1. (c) Scotland and Ireland
2. (a) (d) *Homo erectus* and Neanderthals respectively
3. (b) Marauders from the Aegean and Asia Minor
4. (d) Between 2,047 and 1,940 BC
5. (c) Around AD 100
6. (a) By 6,000 BC
7. (b) (c) Harappa and Mohenjo-Daro
8. (d) 305 BC
9. (c) 1493
10. (d) Mycenaeans

Quiz No 37

1. On the European mainland the Bronze Age preceded which of the following periods, but it did not appear in Britain?
   a. Paleolithic
   b. Mesolithic
   c. Chalcolithic
   d. Neolithic

2. Who colonized the areas outside sub-Saharan Africa around 1.8 million years ago?
   a. Homo erectus
   b. Homo floresiensis
   c. Homo sapiens
   d. Homo heidelbergensis

3. During which of the following periods did the half of the area between the tropics become desert as rainfall diminished?

     a.   Copper Age
     b.   Stone Age
     c.   Iron Age
     d.   Ice Age

4. In which of the following regions were the first large-seeded grasses from which the modern wheat and barley developed, grown?

     a.   Palestine mountain valleys
     b.   Zagros mountain valleys
     c.   Taurus mountain valleys
     d.   All of the above

5. The earliest writings used to preserve the myths became which of these?

     a.   History
     b.   Social Sciences
     c.   Applied Sciences
     d.   Literature

6. Which of these reached India by sea in 1498?

     a.   Vasco de Gama
     b.   Christopher Columbus
     c.   Ferdinand Megellan
     d.   James Cook

7. When did Mayapan become the dominant city of Yucatan?

     a.   1350
     b.   1050
     c.   1250

d. 1150

8. When did a Christian counter-attack drove the Turks out of Hungary?
    a. 1799
    b. 1699
    c. 1499
    d. 1599

9. When did China send the first of seven fleets into the Indian Ocean?
    a. 1505
    b. 1205
    c. 1405
    d. 1305

10. When did Angkor fall to Thai attacks?
    a. After 1369
    b. After 1569
    c. After 1169
    d. After 1269

Answers Quiz 37

1. (c) Chalcolithic or Copper Age (In Britain copper and bronze appeared together)
2. (a) Homo erectus
3. (d) Ice Age
4. (d) Palestine and Zargos and Taurus mountain valleys
5. (a) (b) History and literature
6. (a) Vasco de Gama
7. (c) 1250
8. (b) 1699

9. (c) 1405

10. (a) After 1369

Quiz No 38

1. Larger communal tombs such as long barrows and passage graves and earliest ceremonial monuments known as causewayed enclosures are the signs of which period?
   a. Middle Neolithic
   b. Bronze Age
   c. Chalcolithic
   d. Mesolithic

2. When was the end of the last Ice Age?
   a. 100,000 BC
   b. 100 BC
   c. 10000 BC
   d. 10,000 BC

3. What is the date of the first walled towns in West Asia?
   a. 80,000 BC
   b. 8,000 BC
   c. 80 BC
   d. 800 BC

4. During the 1,700 BC, who overran most of the Egyptian civilization?
   a. Incas
   b. Vikings
   c. Hyksos
   d. Mongols

5. Under whose leadership Egyptian empire was ruled between 1,352 and 1,335 BC?

    a. Cleopatra VII

    b. Amenophis IV

    c. Xerxes I

    d. Djoser

6. When did Chandragupta Maurya conquer the state of Magadha, on the lower Ganges and seized large parts of central India?

    a. 420 BC

    b. 120 BC

    c. 320 BC

    d. 220 BC

7. When did Mycenaeans invade the city of Troy?

    a. 1,250 BC

    b. 1,450 BC

    c. 1,350 BC

    d. 1,050 BC

8. Which of the following is one of the world's earliest urban civilizations?

    a. Inca

    b. Roman

    c. Harappan

    d. Aztec

9. Export trade was established in which of the following items between the Han dynasty of China and Parthia and the Roman Empire?

    a. Silk

    b. Black Pepper

    c. Gold

d. Silver

10. When did a confederation of nomadic tribes from
Mongolia, Hsiung-nu, break through the Great Wall of
China?
a. AD 504
b. AD 304
c. AD 404
d. AD 204

Answers Quiz 38

1. (a) Middle Neolithic
2. (d) 10,000 BC
3. (b) 8,000 BC
4. (c) Asiatic people, Hyksos
5. (b) Amenophis IV and akhenaten
6. (c) 320 BC
7. (a) 1,250 BC
8. (c) Harappan civilization in the Indus valley
9. (a) Silk
10. (b) AD 304

Quiz No 39

1. Larger communal tombs such as long barrow and
passage graves of the Middle Neolithic period were
replaced by what in the Bronze Age?
a. Square barrows
b. Round barrows

    c.   Pentagon barrows

    d.   Diamond barrows

2. By 3,000 BC a power leader created an empire around Upper Egyptian. Where did he establish his new capital which served as the administrative centre for almost 2,000 years?

    a.   Maracanau

    b.   Morocco

    c.   Mesopotamia

    d.   Memphis

3. How many aborigines were living in Australia when Europeans first arrived in the 18th century?

    a.   Up to 200,000

    b.   Up to 20

    c.   Up to 2000

    d.   Up to 20,000

4. When did Sparta declare war on Athens?

    a.   531 BC

    b.   231 BC

    c.   431 BC

    d.   331 BC

5. Which Roman emperor's most of the reign spent on fighting with Parthians and Germans?

    a.   Marcus Aurelius

    b.   Augustus

    c.   Aurelian

    d.   Trajan

6. In AD 325 at Nicaea the Roman Emperor Constantine representing the whole presided over the first ecumenical council. What was the first ecumenical council?

    a.   Defined beliefs for all Germans
    b.   Defined beliefs for all Romans
    c.   Defined beliefs for all Christians
    d.   Defined beliefs for all Parthenians

7.   In AD 597, which mission came to England?

    a.   Augustine of Canterbury
    b.   Saint Patrick
    c.   Saint George
    d.   Paul the Apostle

8.   When did Mongols destroy Baghdad?

    a.   1058
    b.   1258
    c.   1358
    d.   1158

9.   When did the Great Famine spread in northern Europe?

    a.   Between 1515 and 1517
    b.   Between 1215 and 1217
    c.   Between 1315 and 1317
    d.   Between 1415 and 1417

10. Until the 1490s, which of these remained concentrated in Asia and the Americas?

    a.   Negroids
    b.   Mongoloids
    c.   Caucasoids
    d.   Australoids

Answers Quiz 39

1. (b) Round barrows (smaller in size)
2. (d) Memphis
3. (a) Up to 200,000
4. (c) 431 BC
5. (a) Marcus Aurelius (AD 161-180)
6. (c) Defined beliefs for all Christians
7. (a) Augustine of Canterbury
8. (b) 1258
9. (c) Between 1315 and 1317
10. (b) Mongoloids

Quiz No 40

1. What is the Early Bronze Age?
   a. 4500 BC - 3500 BC
   b. 1500 BC - 500 BC
   c. 3500 BC - 2500 BC
   d. 2500 BC - 1500 BC

2. The earliest writings used to keep a record of social customs transformed into which of the following?
   a. Codes of law
   b. Torah
   c. Old Testament
   d. Zabur

3. Trojan War, the legend of invasion of the city Troy by Mycenae empire in 1,250 BC, has been described in which of the renowned poems?

a. Metamorphoses
b. Paradise Lost
c. Iliad
d. Mahabharata

4. When did Rome conquer Sicily after defeating Carthage, the other major power in the western Mediterranean?
   a. 41 BC
   b. 141 BC
   c. 241 BC
   d. 341 BC

5. When did White Huns destroy the Gupta empire of India?
   a. AD 180
   b. AD 280
   c. AD 480
   d. AD 380

6. Under which of the following Byzantine emperors did the Constantinople withstand a four-year siege by Arab armies between AD 674 and 678?
   a. Basil II
   b. Constantine IV
   c. Heraclius
   d. Alexius Comnenus

7. When did the rise of the empire of Mali occur?
   a. 900
   b. 1000
   c. 1200
   d. 1100

8. Who built the magnificent Taj Mahal outside Delhi?

a. Shahjahan

b. Chandragupta Maurya

c. Ranjit Singh

d. Aurangzeb

9. What was the reign of Turkish leader Murad II under which renewal of expansion of Ottoman empire occurred?

a. Between 1013 and 1051

b. Between 1213 and 1251

c. Between 1413 and 1451

d. Between 1113 and 1151

10. When did Incas conquer the Chimu kingdom?

a. 1070

b. 1370

c. 1470

d. 1170

Answers Quiz 40

1. (d) 2500 BC - 1500 BC

2. (a) Codes of law

3. (c) Homer's Iliad

4. (c) 241 BC

5. (c) AD 480

6. (b) Constantine IV

7. (c) 1200

8. (a) Shahjahan

9. (c) Between 1413 and 1451

10. (c) 1470

Quiz No 41

1. What was the Middle Bronze Age?
   a. Between 1600 BC and 1350 BC
   b. Between 1500 BC and 1250 BC
   c. Between 1400 BC and 1150 BC
   d. Between 1300 BC and 1050 BC

2. When were the first ceremonial centres made at Troy in western Anatolia?
   a. 350 BC
   b. 3,350 BC
   c. 2,350 BC
   d. 1,350 BC

3. With whom Greeks came into conflict within the Asia Minor?
   a. Persian Empire
   b. Ottoman Empire
   c. Mughal Empire
   d. Mongol Empire

4. When did the Onin Wars happen and consequently Japan plunged into civil war?
   a. Between 1667 and 1677
   b. Between 1567 and 1577
   c. Between 1367 and 1377
   d. Between 1467 and 1477

5. Who was Shahjahan?
   a. Grandson of Frederick III and fifth Roman emperor
   b. Grandson of Akbar the Great and fifth Mughal emperor

      c.   Grandson of Chandragupta Maurya and fifth Maurya emperor

      d.   Grandson of Genghis Khan and fifth Mongol emperor

6. Who was the ruler of the Islamic World between AD 644 and 656?

      a.   Othman

      b.   Ali

      c.   Abu Bakr

      d.   Umar

7. Missionaries sent by the monastic church of Ireland in the 7th and 8th centuries spread Christianity in which of the following regions?

      a.   Britain

      b.   Europe

      c.   Central Asia

      d.   Africa

8. Originated in Persia, which of the following religions spread extensively in the Roman empire in the form of Mithraism?

      a.   Judaism

      b.   Hinduism

      c.   Zoroastrianism

      d.   Buddhism

9. When was Athens defeated at the hand of Sparta, ending the Peloponnesian war?

      a.   204 BC

      b.   504 BC

      c.   304 BC

      d.   404 BC

10. Until when had at least 16 political units emerged along the Ganges?

    a.   By 600 BC

    b.   By 700 BC

    c.   By 400 BC

    d.   By 500 BC

Answers Quiz 41

1. (b) Between 1500 BC and 1250 BC

2. (c) 2,350 BC

3. (a) Persian Empire

4. (d) Between 1467 and 1477

5. (b) Grandson of Akbar the Great and fifth Mughal emperor

6. (a) Othman

7. (a) (b) Britain and Europe

8. (c) Zoroastrianism

9. (d) 404 BC

10. (a) By 600 BC

Quiz No 42

1. What are the usually accepted dates between the Neolithic and Bronze Age?

    a.   Between 9000 BC and 900 BC

    b.   Between 6000 BC and 600 BC

    c.   Between 8000 BC and 800 BC

    d.   Between 7000 BC and 700 BC

2. What is the date of the first rice cultivation in Yangtze delta, China?

    a.   7,000 BC
    b.   4,000 BC
    c.   5,000 BC
    d.   6,000 BC

3. Rise of which of the following civilizations overshadowed all earlier developments in Mesoamerica about AD 100?

    a.   Teotihuacan
    b.   Olmec
    c.   Zapotec
    d.   Mississippian

4. When was the Gupta dynasty fallen due to barbarian invasions in the subcontinent?

    a.   In the 2nd century
    b.   In the 7th century
    c.   In the 4th century
    d.   In the 5th century

5. Which of the following religions was the first to spread to Japan by the 6th century AD?

    a.   Hinduism
    b.   Buddhism
    c.   Shintoism
    d.   Confucianism

6. Under the Ming dynasty Chinese population reached 100 million. What was the year?

    a.   1460
    b.   1470
    c.   1450
    d.   1440

7. When did a wave of rebel movements begin in China?

    a. 1427

    b. 1727

    c. 1527

    d. 1627

8. What did initiate a duel between Sunnite Ottomans and Shi'ite Persia that lasted for over a century?

    a. Invasion of Sunnite Ottomans

    b. Capture of Tabriz

    c. Invasion of Shi'ite Persia

    d. Capture of Anatolia

9. Where can you find the river Neva, Lake Ladoga, river Volkhov?

    a. Germany

    b. Canada

    c. Russia

    d. Scandinavia

10. Which of the following members of the ruling Umayyad family in Syria seized power in Spain in 755 and made Cordoba his capital and resisted all attempts by the Abbasids to unseat him?

    a. Abu Baker

    b. Abdur Rahman I

    c. Uthman Ibn Affan

    d. Ali Ibn Khattab

Answers Quiz 42

1. (c) Between 8000 BC and 800 BC

2. (d) 6,000 BC

3. (a) Teotihuacan

4. (d) In the 5th century

5. (b) Buddhism

6. (c) 1450

7. (d) 1627

8. (a) (b) Invasion of Sunnite Ottomans under Selim I in 1514 and capture of Tabriz

9. (c) Russia

10. (b) Abdur Rahman I

Quiz No 43

1. When was farming introduced by the Neolithic people in Britain that began a process of radical change?
   a. Around 8,000 years ago
   b. Around 5,000 years ago
   c. Around 6,000 years ago
   d. Around 7,000 years ago

2. When was the first urban civilization grown in the Indus valley?
   a. 500 BC
   b. 1,000 BC
   c. 2,500 BC
   d. 1,500 BC

3. When was the Huari, which was the capital of a state covering most of Peru, abandoned?
   a. AD 500
   b. AD 800
   c. AD 600

d.   AD 700

4. Around 25,000 years ago, which people used to mark
    their sacred places with rock art and had a rich
    symbolic life?
    a.   Aborigines in Australia
    b.   Huli Wigmen, Papua New Guinea
    c.   Himba Herders, Namibia
    d.   Nenet, Siberia

5. Who established the famous cities of Marseilles and
    Naples?
    a.   Phoenicians
    b.   Persians
    c.   Romans
    d.   Mongols

6. Where were the Terracotta warriors discovered in
    1974?
    a.   Tianjin
    b.   Shenzhen
    c.   Beijing
    d.   Xian

7. When did schism between Roman (Catholic) and
    Eastern (Orthodox) churches happen?
    a.   54
    b.   854
    c.   1054
    d.   554

8. Which of the following religions spread from the
    Himalayas in the east to the Atlantic in the west in less
    than a duration of one century?
    a.   Hinduism

b. Islam

c. Jainism

d. Christianity

9. When did Portuguese colonies establish in Angola?

a. 571

b. 1571

c. 3571

d. 2571

10. Under whose leadership Turks captured Constantinople, Moldavia, the Crimea and Trebizond, thereby turning the Black Sea into an Ottoman lake?

a. Osman I

b. Salim I

c. Murad IV

d. Mohammad II

Answers Quiz 43

1. (d) Around 7,000 years ago

2. (c) 2,500 BC

3. (b) AD 800

4. (a) Aborigines in Australia

5. (a) Phoenician or Greeks

6. (d) Near the mausoleum of the first Ch'in emperor, Prince Cheng, in Xian

7. (c) 1054

8. (b) Islam

9. (b) 1571

10. (d) Mohammad II (1451-81)

Quiz No 44

1. Where in Pakistan is one of the two main centres of Indus valley civilization, Harappa, located?
    a. On the Sutlej River in the northeastern sector
    b. On the Ravi River in the northeastern sector
    c. On the Chenab River in the northeastern sector
    d. On the Sindh River in the northeastern sector

2. Chalcolithic period refers to which of these?
    a. Between 1,500 and 100 BC
    b. Between 3,500 and 1,100 BC
    c. Between 4,500 and 2,100 BC
    d. Between 5,500 and 3,100 BC

3. After its greatest extent in 1,340 BC, Mittani territory came under whose control?
    a. Hittite
    b. Assyrian
    c. Inca
    d. Aztec

4. When was Athenian democracy dominated Aegean through the Delian League?
    a. Between 478 and 404 BC
    b. Between 578 and 504 BC
    c. Between 378 and 304 BC
    d. Between 278 and 204 BC

5. Who reached the Americas in 1492?
    a. Marco Polo
    b. James Cook
    c. Christopher Columbus
    d. Vas Code Gama

6. In 1568, who captured Kyoto, the imperial capital of Japan, and by the time he was assassinated in 1582 he had forced almost all the other lords to accept his orders?

    a.   Oda Nobunaga

    b.   Shotoku Taishi

    c.   Sakamoto Ryoma

    d.   Kobo Daishi

7. Which Mongol ruler's troops demolished the fort of Mikrit in the Hindu Kush, and used the defenders' heads to erect a tower of skulls?

    a.   Batu Khan

    b.   Tamerlane

    c.   Kublai Khan

    d.   Genghis Khan

8. Who built the great mosque of Cordoba?

    a.   Suleyman I

    b.   Selim II

    c.   Abdur Rahman I

    d.   Selim I

9. After 1206, which of the following empires were established in Eurasia?

    a.   Persian

    b.   Mughal

    c.   Ottoman

    d.   Mongol

10. When was the Roman empire, that stretched from the Atlantic to the Euphrates and from the English Channel to the Sahara, just a small fortress-town in central Italy commanding both the lowest crossing point on the river

Tiber and a salt route between the mountains and the sea?

    a.   In the 5th century BC

    b.   In the 8th century BC

    c.   In the 6th century BC

    d.   In the 7th century BC

Answers Quiz 44

1. (b) On the Ravi River in the northeastern sector

2. (d) Between 5,500 and 3,100 BC

3. (a) (b) Hittite and Assyrian control

4. (a) Between 478 and 404 BC

5. (c) Christopher Columbus

6. (a) Oda Nobungana, leader of the Oda clan

7. (b) Tamerlane or Timur

8. (c) Abdur Rahman I

9. (d) Mongol

10. (c) In the 6th century BC

Quiz No 45

1.   Under whose command Chinese trading voyages happened between 1405 and 1433?

    a.   Wang Zongyan

    b.   Cheng Ho

    c.   Puyi

    d.   Xizong of Jin

2. Why did the rulers of Egypt construct a series of gigantic pyramid-tombs along the desert edge opposite Memphis during the 'Old Kingdom' (2685-2180 BC)?
    a. To highlight the power and prestige
    b. To highlight the plight and sufferings
    c. To become immorality
    d. To highlight morality

3. When were the mighty Bantu chiefdoms established in southern Africa such as that centred on Great Zimbabwe?
    a. By 14th century
    b. By 11th century
    c. By 13th century
    d. By 12th century

4. When was Alexander the Great the leader of Greek empire?
    a. Between 36 and 23 BC
    b. Between 136 and 123 BC
    c. Between 336 and 323 BC
    d. Between 236 and 223 BC

5. When was Rome invaded by Visigoths?
    a. AD 110
    b. AD 210
    c. AD 310
    d. AD 410

6. When did the popes expand their authority by supporting Christian counter-offensives in Iberia, the Baltic and West Asia which resulted in schism?
    a. After 1254
    b. After 1054
    c. After 1154

    d.   After 154

7.   Which of the following countries chose Catholic Christianity in AD 966 and 1001?
    a.   Russia
    b.   Poland
    c.   Hungary
    d.   Britain

8.   From where did the Umayyad dynasty rule between AD 661 and 750?
    a.   From Mecca in Saudi Arabia
    b.   From Damascus in Syria
    c.   From Tripoli in Libya
    d.   From Cairo in Egypt

9.   In 962, who was coronated as emperor by pope?
    a.   German King Otto 1
    b.   Constantine the Great
    c.   Henry VIII of England
    d.   Charles V of the Holy Roman Empire

10. When did China send the first of seven fleets into the Indian Ocean?
    a.   1305
    b.   1605
    c.   1505
    d.   1405

Answers Quiz 45

1.   (b) Chinese Muslim admiral Cheng Ho
2.   (a) To highlight their power and prestige

3. (c) By 13th century
4. (c) Between 336 and 323 BC
5. (d) AD 410
6. (b) After 1054
7. (b) (c) Poland and Hungary respectively
8. (b) From Damascus in Syria
9. (a) German King Otto 1, Holy Roman Emperor
10. (d) 1405

Quiz No 46

1. Where in Pakistan is one of the two main centres of Indus valley civilization, Mohenjo-Daro, located?
    a. On the Kabul River in the southwestern sector
    b. On the Chenab River in the southwestern sector
    c. On the Indus River in the southwestern sector
    d. On the Jhelum River in the southwestern sector

2. Inhabitants of circular stone-walled huts depended not only on the hunting and herding of gazelle but also, the harvesting of wild wheat. When were these small villages established?
    a. Around 10,000 BC
    b. Around 10 BC
    c. Around 1000 BC
    d. Around 100 BC

3. On which of the following rivers did the prominent cities of Mari and Babylon arise?
    a. Mississippi

b. Euphrates
c. Kwango
d. Tigris

4. When did bronze-working come into use in Europe?
   a. Around 3,500 BC
   b. Around 500 BC
   c. Around 1,500 BC
   d. Around 2,500 BC

5. When was Athenian democracy established as the result of reforms of Cleisthenes?
   a. 5000 BC
   b. 500 BC
   c. 5 BC
   d. 50 BC

6. A census in AD 2 showed some 57 million people living in which of the following empires?
   a. Han dynasty
   b. Abbasid Caliphate
   c. Portuguese Empire
   d. Russian Empire

7. When did missionary Augustine of Canterbury make a voyage to England?
   a. AD 597
   b. AD 697
   c. AD 797
   d. AD 497

8. When were the Magyars of Hungary defeated by German king Otto I at the Battle of Lechfeld?
   a. 1055
   b. 755

    c.   955

    d.   855

9. Which Mughal ruler's reign extended from 1556 and 1605?

    a.   Akbar the Great

    b.   Zahir Uddin Babar

    c.   Aurangzeb Alamgir

    d.   Bahadur Shah Zafar

10. In which of the following centuries did the construction of the transcontinental railways in North America, Siberia and Africa completed?

    a.   In the 17th century

    b.   In the 18th century

    c.   In the 19th century

    d.   In the 20th century

Answers Quiz 46

1. (c) On the Indus River in the southwestern sector

2. (a) Around 10,000 BC

3. (b) Euphrates

4. (d) Around 2,500 BC

5. (b) 500 BC

6. (a) Han dynasty in China

7. (a) AD 597

8. (c) 955

9. (a) Akbar the Great

10. (c) In the 19th century

Quiz No 47

1. Which of the following civilizations lasted no more than 500 years and is much less understood?
   a. Ayyubid caliphate
   b. Indus civilization
   c. Hotak dynasty
   d. Inca empire

2. Where was the cultivation of a cereal millet initiated about 7,000 BC?
   a. Lonesome Valley
   b. Brahmaputra Valley
   c. Loess plain of Yellow River
   d. Hells Canyon

3. What was the period of the Agade empire, which was one of the early empires of Mesopotamia?
   a. Between 3,296 and 3,105 BC
   b. Between 296 and 105 BC
   c. Between 1,296 and 1,105 BC
   d. Between 2,296 and 2,105 BC

4. When was New Zealand first colonized?
   a. Between AD 750 and 1,300
   b. Between AD 850 and 1,400
   c. Between AD 650 and 1,200
   d. Between AD 550 and 1,100

5. When did the reign of King Samudragupta begin in the Subcontinent?
   a. AD 135
   b. AD 235
   c. AD 335

d.   AD 435

6. Which of the following is the greatest of all missionary religions?

    a.   Confucianism

    b.   Shintoism

    c.   Jainism

    d.   Buddhism

7. When did the Roman empire annex Carthage and Corinth?

    a.   146 BC

    b.   246 BC

    c.   346 BC

    d.   46 BC

8. When did the Han Empire collapse?

    a.   AD 500

    b.   AD 100

    c.   AD 300

    d.   AD 200

9. After the crushing victory of the Seljuk Turks over Byzantine forces in 1071 which of the following Byzantine emperors called on the west for help that started the sequence of events that led to the First Crusade between 1096 and 1099?

    a.   Irene

    b.   Diocletian

    c.   Alexius I

    d.   Justinian

10. In 800, the pope in Rome crowned whom the emperor of the west?

    a.   Charlemagne

b.   Frederick I
c.   Frederick II
d.   Maximillian I

Answers Quiz 47

1.   (b) Indus civilization of Pakistan
2.   (c) Loess plain of Yellow River, northern China
3.   (d) Between 2,296 and 2,105 BC
4.   (a) Between AD 750 and 1,300
5.   (c) AD 335
6.   (d) Buddhism
7.   (a) 146 BC
8.   (b) AD 100
9.   (c) Emperor Alexius I (1081-1118)
10. (b) Charles the Great or Charlemagne (768-814)

Quiz No 48

1.   Who was told that 400,000 men a year, working in three months relays, had been engaged for 10 years in constructing the causeway and platform for the Great Pyramid, and another 20 years on the pyramid itself?
     a.   Livy
     b.   Thucydides
     c.   Herodotus
     d.   Bede

2.   Which of these ended the 'Dark Age' period spanning between 1,200 and 900 BC?

    a. Phoenicians
    b. Assyrians
    c. Carthaginians
    d. Incas

3. Where was the Hindu religion, a Sanskrit literature, a caste system and iron working, emerged between 1,500 and 800 BC?
    a. Indus Valley
    b. South East Asia
    c. Central Asia
    d. Western Asia

4. Which of the following religions thrived with the Chinese empire of Chou?
    a. Jainism
    b. Confucianism
    c. Hinduism
    d. Taoism

5. When was Jesus of Nazareth, the founder of Christianity, executed?
    a. AD 29
    b. AD 2
    c. AD 9
    d. AD 18

6. When did the Muslims cross over the Straits of Gibraltar and conquered Spain?
    a. AD 811
    b. AD 511
    c. AD 711
    d. AD 611

7. Why is Africa called the 'dark continent'?

    a.   Because in 1900, Africa remained independent of foreign control: a world unto itself

    b.   Because in 1800, Africa remained independent of foreign control: a world unto itself

    c.   Because in 1500, Africa remained independent of foreign control: a world unto itself

    d.   Because in 1600, Africa remained independent of foreign control: a world unto itself

8. When did Europe experience the first of many famines?
    a.   Between 1315 and 1317
    b.   Between 1515 and 1517
    c.   Between 1415 and 1417
    d.   Between 1215 and 1217

9. In which of the following centuries did the Suez Canal open?
    a.   In the 17th century
    b.   In the 20th century
    c.   In the 18th century
    d.   In the 19th century

10. When did Dutch establish Cape Colony?
    a.   1752
    b.   1452
    c.   1652
    d.   1552

Answers Quiz 48

1. (c) The Greek historian Herodotus when he visited Egypt in the fifth century B.C.

2. (b) Assyrians

3. (a) (b) Indus valley, South East Asia
4. (b) (d) Confucianism and Taoism
5. (a) AD 29
6. (c) AD 711
7. (b) Because in 1800, Africa remained independent of foreign control: a world unto itself
8. (a) Between 1315 and 1317
9. (d) In the 19th century
10. (c) 1652

Quiz No 49

1. Where did the first civilizations emerge?
   a. Lower Tigris and Euphrates valleys
   b. Valley of the Nile
   c. Indus valley around Harappa and Mohenjo-Daro
   d. Yellow River around An-yang
   e. All of the above

2. In the 9th century BC which powerful Assyrian leader built a glorious palace at Nimrud?
   a. Tiglath Pileser I
   b. Ashurnasirpal II
   c. Enlil Nirari
   d. Shalmaneser I

3. What do Gautam Buddha, the founder of Buddhism, and Mahavira, the founder of Jainism, share in common?
   a. Born in the 7th century along the Tigris valleys
   b. Born in the 4th century along the Nile valleys

    c.   Born in the 5th century along the Indus valleys

    d.   Born in the 6th century along the Ganges valleys

4. When was there a Jewish rebellion against the Roman empire?
- a. 64 BC
- b. 6 BC
- c. 10 BC
- d. 4 BC

5. During which of the following centuries did the alliances of several nomadic tribes launch devastating attacks on all the big empires in the world?
- a. In the 1st and 2nd centuries AD
- b. In the 2nd and 3rd centuries AD
- c. In the 4th and 5th centuries AD
- d. In the 3rd and 4th centuries AD

6. When did Seljuk Turks establish themselves in Anatolia after driving out Christians?
- a. 1155
- b. 855
- c. 1055
- d. 955

7. Which of the following areas did the conquerors impose Christianity?
- a. In the Africa and Australia
- b. In the Americas and Philippines
- c. In the South Asia and New Zealand
- d. In the Middle East and Russia

8. When was the foundation of Angkor laid down in Cambodia?

a. 802
b. 902
c. 602
d. 702

9. Which of the following were the Mongol states?
    a. Golden Horde
    b. Il-Khans
    c. Chagatai
    d. All of the above

10. When did the Umayyad dynasty rule from Damascus in Syria?
    a. Between AD 861 and 950
    b. Between AD 561 and 650
    c. Between AD 761 and 850
    d. Between AD 661 and 750

Answers Quiz 49

1. (e) The lower Tigris and Euphrates valleys; the valley of the Nile; the Indus valley around Harappa and Mohenjo-Daro; and the Yellow River around An-yang
2. (b) Ashurnasirpal II (883-859 BC)
3. (d) Born in the 6th century along the Ganges valleys
4. (a) 64 BC
5. (c) In the 4th and 5th centuries AD
6. (c) 1055
7. (b) In the Americas and Philippines
8. (a) 802
9. (d) All of the above
10. (d) Between AD 661 and 750

Quiz No 50

1. Which of these was the literate class in the first civilizations?
   a. Donor class
   b. Priesthood
   c. Gentry
   d. Corporate class

2. Which powerful leader conquered Babylonia and occupied the Phoenician cities on the Mediterranean coast?
   a. Erisham I
   b. Tiglathpileser III
   c. Sargon II
   d. Puzuashure II

3. Which of the following is one of Asia's most pervasive religions?
   a. Shintoism
   b. Judaism
   c. Buddhism
   d. Zoroastrianism

4. Who is the founder of mystical religion Tao or 'the Way'?
   a. Lao-Tzu
   b. Mahavira
   c. Pythagoras
   d. Saicho

5. What do the Roman empire, Han dynasty and the Persian empire share in common?

a. Three largest empires in the world established during the 2nd century AD
b. Three largest empires in the world established during the 3rd century AD
c. Three largest empires in the world established during the 5ft century AD
d. Three largest empires in the world established during the 4th century AD

6. According to the AD 2 census, where in the world were population densities reached 150 per square mile?
   a. Around Yellow River plain in Han dynasty
   b. Around Sindh River plain in Kusan dynasty
   c. Around Ganges River plain in Maurya dynasty
   d. Around Nile River plain in Tenth dynasty

7. When did the Greek empire re-establish?
   a. 1061
   b. 1161
   c. 1261
   d. 1361

8. When did Vladimir of Kiev convert to Christianity?
   a. 687
   b. 987
   c. 887
   d. 787

9. In South-East Asia, first the Mongols and then the Shans sacked which civilization in the 13th century?
   a. Toungoo
   b. Aceh
   c. Khmer
   d. Pagan

10. Until the 1490s, which of these remained concentrated in Europe, North Africa, the Middle East and India?
    a. Negroids
    b. Mongoloids
    c. Caucasoids
    d. Australoids

Answers Quiz 50

1. (b) Usually the priesthood
2. (c) Sargon II (721-705 BC)
3. (c) Buddhism
4. (a) Lao-Tzu
5. (b) Three largest empires in the world established during the 3rd century AD
6. (a) Around Yellow River plain in Han dynasty
7. (c) 1261
8. (b) 987
9. (d) Kingdom of Pagan
10. (c) Caucasoids

Quiz No 51

1. When did our genus *Homo* (man) begin to undergo important evolutionary trends, acquiring a larger brain and full bipedalism?
    a. About 4 million years ago
    b. About 1 million years ago
    c. About 2 million years ago
    d. About 3 million years ago

2. When were the dynasties of XVIIIth and XIXth flourishing in Egypt?

    a.   Between 1470 and 1100 BC

    b.   Between 1670 and 1300 BC

    c.   Between 1570 and 1200 BC

    d.   Between 570 and 200 BC

3. Which of the following kingdoms emerged around 900 BC?

    a.   Kingdom of Meroe

    b.   Ming dynasty

    c.   Clan of the Great Khan

    d.   House of Platagenet

4. When was the Battle of Chaeronea fought in which Philip II of Macedon achieved control of Greece?

    a.   138 BC

    b.   238 BC

    c.   438 BC

    d.   338 BC

5. Prince Cheng of Ch'in dynasty who came into power in 221 BC, introduced a uniform coinage whose distinctive shape circular with a square hole in the centre remained standard until when?

    a.   1911

    b.   1711

    c.   1311

    d.   1511

6. After the barbarian invasion of the 4th and 5th centuries, how did the Sui dynasty (581-617) succeed to establish its empire and reunify China?

    a.   Because of standardized institutions

     b.   Because of a state-sponsored broad-based Buddhism

     c.   Because of the construction of a canal system linking the Yangtze with the Yellow River and the Lo-yang region

     d.   All of the above

7. When did Seljuk Turks gain a crushing victory over Byzantine Empire at Manzikert?
- a.   171
- b.   1071
- c.   971
- d.   71

8. When was Grand Prince Svyatoslav ruler in Kievan Russia?
- a.   Between 662 and 672
- b.   Between 762 and 772
- c.   Between 962 and 972
- d.   Between 862 and 872

9. When was the growth of the Inca empire?
- a.   Between 1538 and 1625
- b.   Between 1238 and 1325
- c.   Between 1338 and 1425
- d.   Between 1438 and 1525

10. In Laos, which new political centre replaced the old temple cities?
- a.   Luang Prabang
- b.   Vientiane
- c.   Sikhottabong
- d.   Wat Phu

Answers Quiz 51

1. (d) About 3 million years ago
2. (c) Between 1570 and 1200 BC
3. (a) Kingdom of Meroe
4. (d) 338 BC
5. (a) 1911
6. (d) All of the above
7. (b) 1071
8. (c) Between 962 and 972
9. (d) Between 1438 and 1525
10. (a) Luang Prabang (1353)

Quiz No 52

1. What was a central part of hominine's diet around 2.5 million years ago?
    a. Salad
    b. Meat
    c. Cereals
    d. Rice

2. Among the first civilizations, how were the institutions such as the legal system, army, bureaucracy developed and the division of society into different segments taken place?
    a. Due to the existence of devolved control in these societies
    b. Due to the existence of centralised control in these societies

     c.   Due to the existence of nomadic nature of these societies

     d.   Due to the existence of priesthood in these societies

3. What is the period known as when many abandoned districts of Maya kingdoms were regenerated?

     a.   Pre-Classic
     b.   Classic
     c.   Post-Classic
     d.   None of the above

4. When were the major cities of Harappa and Mohenjo-Daro culture abandoned in the Indus valley?

     a.   About AD750
     b.   About 750 BC
     c.   About 2,750 BC
     d.   About 1,750 BC

5. Due to Phoenician exploration and settlement, when was the emergence of the first monumental public buildings, a new alphabet, changes in burial practices, and new artistic styles materialized in the Mediterranean world?

     a.   Around 9th century BC
     b.   Around 6th century BC
     c.   Around 8th century BC
     d.   Around 7th century BC

6. Under the leadership of Alaric, when did Visigoths capture Rome?

     a.   AD 410
     b.   AD 110
     c.   AD 210
     d.   AD 310

7. When was Constantinople defeated by the Fourth Crusade and the Latin empire established?
    a.   904
    b.   1204
    c.   1104
    d.   1004

8. When did Pippin III usurp Frankish throne and became first king of the Carolingian dynasty?
    a.   551
    b.   651
    c.   851
    d.   751

9. When was the grandson of Genghis Khan, Kublai Khan, leader of the Mongols?
    a.   Between 1260 and 1294
    b.   Between 1360 and 1394
    c.   Between 1460 and 1494
    d.   Between 1160 and 1194

10. When did descendants of Tamerlane/Timur, Babur, conquer Delhi Sultanate and founded Mughal empire?
    a.   1326
    b.   1626
    c.   1426
    d.   1526

Answers Quiz 52

1. (b) Meat

2. (b) Due to the existence of centralised control in these societies
3. (c) Post-Classic
4. (d) About 1,750 BC
5. (c) Around 8th century BC
6. (a) AD 410
7. (b) 1204
8. (d) 751
9. (a) Between 1260 and 1294
10. (d) In 1526 Battle of Panipat

Quiz No 53

1. How long ago had hominines learnt to cook their food, indicated by burnt bones found in southern Africa?
   a. 1.0 million years
   b. 2.5 million years
   c. 0.5 million years
   d. 1.5 million years

2. Which king of the Agade empire left rock-reliefs to commemorate his achievements near Diyarbakir in Turkey and in the Zagros?
   a. Rimush
   b. Sargon
   c. Naram Sin of Agade
   d. Manishtusu

3. When did Gupta dynasty rule large parts of the subcontinent extending from Indus to the Bay of Bengal?
   a. By AD 400

b. By AD 100

c. By AD 200

d. By AD 300

4. When did the teachings of Zoroaster emerge?

    a. Around 1,400 BC

    b. Around 1,000 BC

    c. Around 200 BC

    d. Around 1,200 BC

5. After AD 500, when nomads from the Asian steppes had sacked the narrow chain of empires extending from Rome to China, which of the following two phenomena dominated in Eurasia?

    a. Growth of Islam after AD 632

    b. Establishment of the Mongol empire after AD 1206

    c. Establishment of the Mughal empire after AD 1526

    d. Enlightenment movement in 17th and 18th centuries

6. When did the early Abbasid Caliphate rule the Islamic civilization?

    a. Between 550 and 650

    b. Between 650 and 750

    c. Between 750 and 850

    d. Between 850 and 950

7. The Mughals were the descendants of whom?

    a. Babur

    b. Alamgir

    c. Shahjahan

    d. Akbar

8. When was the Ming dynasty toppled and Manchus invaded China?
   a. 1744
   b. 1644
   c. 1444
   d. 1544

9. When did Pizarro begin the conquest of Inca empire?
   a. 1731
   b. 1631
   c. 1431
   d. 1531

10. Extinction of Neanderthals?
    a. 3,000 BC
    b. 120 BC
    c. 12,000 BC
    d. 1200 BC

Answers Quiz 53

1. (d) 1.5 million years
2. (c) Naram Sin of Agade (2213-2176 BC)
3. (a) By AD 400
4. (d) Around 1,200 BC
5. (a) (b) The growth of Islam after AD 632 and the establishment of the Mongol empire after AD 1206
6. (c) Between 750 and 850
7. (a) Babur - a descendant of Timur/Tamerlane
8. (b) 1644
9. (d) 1531
10. (c) 12,000 BC

Quiz No 54

1. Which development did aid hominies in the digestion of their food around 1.5 million years ago?
   a. Learned to break down animal proteins before eating by cooking their food
   b. Learned to break down animal proteins before eating by cooling their food
   c. Learned to break down animal proteins before eating by making small pieces of their food
   d. Learned to break down animal proteins before eating by storing their food

2. Akkadian was the main language of Mesopotamia after replacing Sumerian. What other languages emanated from Akkadian?
   a. Farsi
   b. Babylonian
   c. Assyrian
   d. Dravidian

3. Which civilization ended in AD 850 in Mesoamerica?
   a. Assyrian
   b. Inca
   c. Aztec
   d. Mayan

4. When were the first Phoenician exploration and settlements expanded to the north and east Africa along the Black Sea coast?
   a. By the middle of the 7th century
   b. By the middle of the 6th century
   c. By the middle of the 5th century
   d. By the middle of the 4th century

5. Which of the following officers of Alexander the Great is renowned for his voyage and exploration of the Indian Ocean and the Persian Gulf?
   a. Perdiccas
   b. Cleitus
   c. Nearchus
   d. Hephaestion

6. When was bronze technology, animal power and irrigation system introduced in China, increasing both food production and population?
   a. In the 7th century BC
   b. In the 4th century BC
   c. In the 6th century BC
   d. In the 5th century BC

7. Which of the following ecumenical councils ventured to impose orthodoxy on the Christian world held in AD 451?
   a. First council of Nicaea
   b. Council of Chalcedon
   c. First council of Nicaea
   d. Second council of Constantinople

8. When did Cortes begin the conquest of Aztec empire?
   a. 1619
   b. 1419
   c. 1519
   d. 1319

9. When did the Union of Poland and Lithuania take place?
   a. 1486
   b. 1186

    c. 1286
    d. 1386

10. Which conflict - that lasted for over a century - centred
    around the key cities of Mesopotamia, and Baghdad,
    Tiflis, Derbend and Basra changed hands repeatedly?
    a. Greeks vs Romans
    b. Sunnite Ottomans vs Shi'ite Persia
    c. Mongols vs Abbasid Caliphate
    d. Catholics vs Protestants

Answers Quiz 53

1. (a) Learned to break down animal proteins before
    eating by cooking their food
2. (b) (c) Babylonian and Assyrian
3. (d) Mayan
4. (b) By the middle of the sixth century (Around 550 BC)
5. (c) Nearchus
6. (d) In the 5th century BC
7. (b) Council of Chalcedon
8. (c) 1519
9. (d) 1386
10. (b) Sunnite Ottomans and Shi'ite Persia, initiated when
    Sunnite Ottomans under Salim I invaded Persia in 1514
    and captured Tabriz

Quiz No 54

1. What had all three - *Homo erectus, Homo heidelbergensis, Homo ergaster* - in common?
   a. All three had learned cooking food before eating
   b. All three had developed centralized societies
   c. All three had brains of about 1,000 cubic centimeters
   d. All three had adaptable stone technology

2. Where were the earliest readable documents found which dated back to ....?
   a. Jerusalem, 4,200 BC
   b. Rome, 1,200 BC
   c. Cairo, 2,200 BC
   d. Mesopotamia, 3,200 BC

3. When were lowland kingdoms of Maya developing?
   a. About AD 400
   b. About AD 300
   c. About AD 100
   d. About AD 200

4. Between AD 300 and 550, which of the following civilizations were formed in the Subcontinent?
   a. Gupta-Vakataka
   b. Maurya
   c. Mughal
   d. British Raj

5. Which of the following religions does not believe in the existence of a god as it emphasises on getting out of sufferings through the ending of your desires?
   a. Jainism
   b. Hinduism
   c. Buddhism

d. Judaism

6. When did the Ming dynasty take power in China?
    a. 1468
    b. 1368
    c. 1568
    d. 1268

7. In 1739, who invaded India and sacked Delhi, leaving the Mughal empire fatally weakened?
    a. Alexander the Great
    b. Zahir Uddin Babur
    c. Sundara Pandya
    d. Nadir Shah

8. In 862, the Slavs called whom to protect them from Pechenga raiders from Asia?
    a. Vikings
    b. Mongols
    c. Turks
    d. Mughals

9. In AD 313, the new faith of toleration, Edict of Milan, was granted by which of the following Roman emperors?
    a. Rudolf II
    b. Maximilian I
    c. Constantine
    d. Charlemagne

10. What is the series of three wars fought between Roman and Carthage empire between 264 and 146 BC, known as?
    a. Wars of the Diadochi
    b. Punic wars

c. Crusades

d. Battle of Roses

Answers Quiz 54

1. (c) (d) All three had brains of about 1,000 cubic centimeters and adaptable stone technology
2. (d) Mesopotamia, 3,200 BC
3. (c) About AD 100
4. (a) Gupta-Vakataka empire
5. (c) Buddhism
6. (b) 1368
7. (d) Nadir Shah
8. (a) Rurik the Vikings
9. (c) Emperor Constantine
10. (b) Punic wars

Quiz No 55

1. How long ago did regional populations such as Neanderthals develop through many dispersals of populations and much intermingling of genes?
   a. About 500 years
   b. About 5,000 years
   c. About 50,000 years
   d. About 500,000 years

2. During whose reign the Egyptian empire stretched through Palestine into Syria?
   a. Khufu

b.   Ramesses II

c.   Neferkara I

d.   Djoser

3.   Signed in AD 313, in which of the following documents proclaimed tolerance for all religions in the Roman empire?

a.   Edict of Milan

b.   Emancipation Proclamation

c.   Gutenberg Bible

d.   Magna Carta

4.   What do all the world religions, to some degree, share in common?

a.   A belief in a single spiritual reality

b.   All religions were born in Middle East

c.   All religions were born in Northern Africa

d.   All religions were born in South America

5.   Which of the following dynasties replaced the first dynasty of China, the Shang?

a.   Sui

b.   Chou

c.   Tang

d.   Qin

6.   In the reign of which of the following Roman emperors was the first full ecclesiastical organisation established?

a.   Constantine

b.   Charlemagne

c.   Frederick I

d.   Maximilian I

7.   When did Seljuk Turks establish themselves in Baghdad?

      a.   1355
      b.   1255
      c.   1155
      d.   1055

8. When did Aztec expansion begin?
      a.   1528
      b.   1228
      c.   1328
      d.   1428

9. In 1368, who claimed himself the founder of a new imperial dynasty, taking the title Hung-wu, meaning 'mighty martial'?
      a.   Wang Mang
      b.   Wanli Emperor
      c.   Wu Zentian
      d.   Chu Yuan-chang

10. When did Mongols attack Vladimir-Suzdal?
      a.   From 1237 to 1238
      b.   From 1437 to 1438
      c.   From 1337 to 1338
      d.   From 1137 to 1138

Answers Quiz 55

1. (d) About 500,000 years
2. (b) Ramesses II (1290-1224 BC)
3. (a) Edict of Milan
4. (a) A belief in a single spiritual reality
5. (b) Chou dynasty
6. (a) Emperor Constantine

7. (d) 1055
8. (d) 1428
9. (d) Chu Yuan-chang
10. (a) From 1237 to 1238

Quiz No 56

1. How long ago did anatomically modern people - *Homo sapiens* - emigrate from sub-Saharan Africa?
   a. About 10 years
   b. About 1,000 years
   c. About 10,000 years
   d. About 100,000 years

2. The earliest of all known civilizations, Sumer, comprised about 12 city-states in northern Mesopotamia. What was the size of the largest of them all?
   a. Walled of around 100 hectares where some 30,000 people resided
   b. Walled of around 50 hectares where some 3,000 people resided
   c. Walled of around 10 hectares where some 300 people resided
   d. Walled of around 1,000 hectares where some 300,000 people resided

3. By 800 BC, who had established complex settlements at Monte Alban with the population reaching up to tens of thousands?
   a. Aztec
   b. Olmec

c. Zapotec

d. Maya

4. During the 4th and 5th centuries, which of the following nomadic groups swept south-westwards through Asia, initiating a chain reaction among the Germanic people along the Black Sea and the Danube?

a. Kochi

b. Huns

c. Bedouin

d. Maasai

5. Which of the following was a new capital of the Sung dynasty, established between AD 960 and 1279, that became the world's largest city?

a. Hang-chou

b. K'ai-feng

c. Luoyang

d. Nanjing

6. When did Muslims finally defeat the Persian empire at Merv?

a. AD 851

b. AD 551

c. AD 751

d. AD 651

7. The chalcolithic period is further divided into which of the following?

a. Ubaid period

b. Paleolithic period

c. Neolithic period

d. Uruk period

8. When was the Pueblo culture in North America on its height?
   a. 1000
   b. 1300
   c. 1100
   d. 1200

9. When did the Ottomans take Edirne (Adrianople), which became their new capital?
   a. 1261
   b. 1561
   c. 1461
   d. 1361

10. Lithuania united in 1386 with which country to form the largest state in Eastern Europe?
    a. Poland
    b. Hungary
    c. Austria
    d. Switzerland

Answers Quiz 56

1. (d) About 100,000 years ago
2. (a) Walled of around 100 hectares where some 30,000 people resided
3. (c) Zapotec
4. (b) The Huns
5. (a) Hang-chou
6. (d) AD 651
7. (a) (d) Ubaid period and Uruk period
8. (c) 1100
9. (d) 1361

10. (a) Poland

Quiz No 57

1. How long ago were the Americas reached?
- a. By 16,000 years
- b. By 15,000 years
- c. By 14,000 years
- d. By 13,000 years

2. Where was the cereal rice first cultivated in 6,000 BC?
- a. Yangtze valley
- b. Nile valley
- c. Amazon valley
- d. Sindh valley

3. When did Amorite Shamshi-Adad become the Assyrian king?
- a. 1,549 BC
- b. 1,649 BC
- c. 1,749 BC
- d. 1,849 BC

4. Which of the following cities conquered in 1,250 by Mycenaeans was strategically important as it was located at the entrance to Dardanelles and controlled access to the trade of the Black Sea?
- a. Gaziantep
- b. Byblos
- c. Luxor
- d. Troy

5. Which of the following religions was originally born as a result of reformist movement within Hinduism?

    a.   Shintoism

    b.   Buddhism

    c.   Zoroastrianism

    d.   Judaism

6. Out of seven states competing for hegemony over China, only one was left by 221 BC. Which one was that?

    a.   Wei

    b.   Yan

    c.   Han

    d.   Ch'in

7. When did the Vandals, Alans and Sueves invade the Gaul region of Western Europe?

    a.   AD 306

    b.   AD 606

    c.   AD 406

    d.   AD 506

8. Followers of which of the following religions are found scattered from Morocco to Indonesia, and Siberia to Zanzibar?

    a.   Islam

    b.   Judaism

    c.   Shintoism

    d.   Hinduism

9. Which prominent Asiatic nomadic tribes assaulted the first Russian state, Kievan Russia?

    a.   Varangians

    b.   Pechenegs

    c.   Polovtsy

    d.   Vladimir Monokhov

10. Which disease killed around 20 million Europeans between 1346 and 1353?
    a.   Black Death
    b.   Spanish flu
    c.   Yellow fever
    d.   Polio

Answers Quiz 57

1.   (b) By 15,000 years
2.   (a) Yangtze valley, southern China
3.   (c) 1,749 BC
4.   (d) Troy - recorded in the Homer's Iliad as the legend of Trojan War
5.   (b) Buddhism
6.   (d) Ch'in or Qin
7.   (c) AD 406
8.   (a) Islam
9.   (b) (c) Pechenegs and Polovtsy
10. (a) Black Death or bubonic plague

Quiz No 58

1.   How long ago were the major expansions in the Arctic begun as the continental ice sheets retreated?
    a.   About 2,500 years
    b.   About 1,500 years
    c.   About 3,500 years

      d.   About 4,500 years

2. Why were the first civilizations emerged from the basin of four major rivers: Tigris and Euphrates in Mesopotamia, the Nile in Egypt, Yellow River in China, and Indus in Pakistan?
   - a.   Because people around these rivers had more developed brains
   - b.   Because farming began around the mountain where these rivers drain
   - c.   Because hunting began around these rivers drain due to animal density
   - d.   Because jungles began growing around where these rivers drain

3. When did humans move from Asia into North America using the dried out Bering Strait?
   - a.   Around 10,000 BC
   - b.   Around 5,000 BC
   - c.   Around 20,000 BC
   - d.   Around 15,000 BC

4. When did iron come into use in Southeast Asia?
   - a.   About 600 BC
   - b.   About 1000 BC
   - c.   About 500 BC
   - d.   About 400 BC

5. How did the spread of great religions play an important role?
   - a.   People became more faithful and religious
   - b.   People more peaceful and learned
   - c.   Different areas of the world were linked
   - d.   Values of advanced cultures spread to far off areas of the world

6. When was the first emperor, Prince Cheng of the Ch'in dynasty ruled on China?
   a. Between 221 and 206 BC
   b. Between 201 and 186 BC
   c. Between 241 and 226 BC
   d. Between 231 and 216 BC

7. When was Russian prince Vladimir baptized and Orthodox Christianity spread in Russia?
   a. AD 988
   b. AD 788
   c. AD 1088
   d. AD 888

8. Which of the following dynasties created a new capital at Baghdad in Mesopotamia and opened government to non-Arab Muslims (known as mawali)?
   a. Abbasid
   b. Mughal
   c. Maurya
   d. Ottoman

9. Until when had the followers of Rurik the Vikings occupied the Smolensk, Dnieper and Kiev in Russia?
   a. 982
   b. 682
   c. 782
   d. 882

10. Which empire's achievements depended absolutely upon the acquiescence of the 150 million or so Hindu peasant farmers and petty landlords who paid the taxes that supported the empire's 4 million warriors, and the court grandees who commanded them?

a. Persian
b. Mughal
c. Roman
d. Mongol

Answers Quiz 58

1. (d) About 4,500 years
2. (b) Because farming began around the mountain where these rivers drain
3. (d) Around 15,000 BC
4. (c) About 500 BC
5. (c) (d) Different areas of the world were linked and values of advanced cultures spread to far off areas of the world
6. (a) Between 221 and 206 BC
7. (a) AD 988
8. (a) Abbasid
9. (d) 882
10. (b) Mughal empire in subcontinent

Quiz No 59

1. How long ago did humans reach New Zealand?
    a. Around 1,200 years
    b. Around 1,600 years
    c. Around 1,400 years
    d. Around 1,000 years

2. Which of the following was a Babylonian king who stretched and strengthened the Babylonian empire?
    a. Genghis Khan
    b. Alexander the Great
    c. Nebuchadnezzar
    d. Attila the Hun

3. Theravada is the conservative form of which of the following religions?
    a. Buddhism
    b. Zoroastrianism
    c. Judaism
    d. Shintoism

4. When did Rome conquer Spain after defeating Carthage, the other major power in the western Mediterranean?
    a. 6 BC
    b. 306 BC
    c. 106 BC
    d. 206 BC

5. After AD 500, when nomads from the Asian steppes had sacked the narrow chain of empires extending from Rome to China, which of the following empires grew in Africa?
    a. Empire of Ghana
    b. Empire of Mali
    c. Empire of Songhai
    d. All of the above

6. In 1387, which of the following was the last remaining pagan state in Europe that opted for Catholicism?
    a. Poland
    b. Lithuania

c. Russia

d. Germany

7. According to religion of Islam, following the split of Ali, the Prophet Muhammad (PBUH)'s cousin and son-in-law (the Shi'ites), the majority of Muslims accepted the rule of which of the following dynasty who claimed to represent the Sunna or traditions of the Prophet?

    a. Seljuk

    b. Ottoman

    c. Umayyad

    d. Abbasid

8. Who conquered Sicily in 1194?

    a. Emperor Henry VI

    b. Charlemagne

    c. Constantine the Great

    d. Julius Caesar

9. Which Great Khan of the Mongols spent most of his long reign (1260-94) seeking to reunify China and conquer Japan?

    a. Kublai Khan

    b. Genghis Khan

    c. Ogedei

    d. Tamerlane

10. In 1274/1281, whose invasions of Japan were defeated?

    a. Mongol

    b. Ottoman

    c. Mughal

    d. Abbasid

Answers Quiz 59

1. (a) Around 1,200 years
2. (c) Nebuchadnezzar (604-562 BC)
3. (a) Buddhism
4. (d) 206 BC
5. (a) (b) (c) All of the above, The empires of Ghana, Mali and Songhai
6. (b) Lithuania
7. (c) Umayyad dynasty
8. (a) Emperor Henry VI
9. (a) Kublai Khan
10. (a) Mongol

Quiz No 60

1. According to DNA studies, how long ago did the first anatomically modern humans (*Homo sapiens sapiens*) arise?
   a. Between 50,000 and 20,000 years
   b. Between 300,000 and 240,000 years
   c. Between 100,000 and 40,000 years
   d. Between 200,000 and 140,000 years

2. Where is a developed Neolithic excavation site, Catal Huyuk, located?
   a. Anatolia, Turkey
   b. Cairo, Egypt
   c. Amman, Jordan
   d. Damascus, Syria

3. Which of the following Assyrian leaders conquered Memphis and annexed Thebes, however, did not establish formalized control over Egypt?

    a.   Samani

    b.   Mandaru

    c.   Esarhaddon

    d.   Ashurbanipal

4. The graphics pottery of the Moche, for which the coast of the central Andes is known, dates back?

    a.   Between AD 200 and 700

    b.   Between AD 100 and 600

    c.   Between AD 50 and 555

    d.   Between AD 1 and 500

5. Which civilization in Europe created a script known as Linear A in about 1,600 BC?

    a.   Minoan

    b.   Mycenaean

    c.   Venetian

    d.   Genoese

6. Which of the following religions first spread throughout India then on to Sri Lanka, Burma, Thailand and South-East Asia?

    a.   Buddhism

    b.   Islam

    c.   Christianity

    d.   Shintoism

7. After defeating which of the following empires, the Roman empire annexed Macedon, Greece and Western Anatolia?

    a.   Visigoth

    b.   Phoenician

        c.   Hellenistic
        d.   Carthaginian

8.   When did a confederation of nomadic tribes from
     Mongolia, Hsiung-nu, invade the capital of the ancient
     Han dynasty, Chang'an?
        a.   AD 416
        b.   AD 116
        c.   AD 216
        d.   AD 316

9.   Which of the following countries chose Orthodox
     Christianity in AD 988?
        a.   Russia
        b.   Poland
        c.   Hungary
        d.   Britain

10. Which of the following books is a volume of
     prescriptions on behaviour as well as belief?
        a.   Vedas
        b.   Koran
        c.   Agamas
        d.   Kajaki

Answers Quiz 60

1.   (d) Between 200,000 and 140,000 years
2.   (a) Anatolia, Turkey
3.   (c) Esarhaddon (680-669 BC) and Ashurbanipal (668-
     627 BC)
4.   (b) Between AD 100 and 600
5.   (a) Minoan culture

6. (a) Buddhism

7. (c) Hellenistic kingdoms

8. (d) AD 316

9. (a) Russia

10. (b) Koran

Quiz No 61

1. When did the Umayyad dynasty flourish?

    a. Between AD 561 and 650

    b. Between AD 661 and 750

    c. Between AD 761 and 850

    d. Between AD 861 and 950

2. When was Vladimir's Svyatostav ruler in Kievan Russia?

    a. Between 770 and 815

    b. Between 1080 and 1115

    c. Between 980 and 1015

    d. Between 880 and 915

3. When did Mongol ruler, Timur or Tamerlane, defeated the Ottoman empire at the battle of Ankara?

    a. 1402

    b. 1102

    c. 1502

    d. 1302

4. Which city became the capital of a new Mon kingdom in the south in the South-East Asia region?

    a. Luang Prabang

    b. Pegu

c.   Ava

d.   Chiang Mai

5. By when, had the Turks crossed the Dardanelles to
     Gallipoli?

     a.   1454

     b.   1154

     c.   1254

     d.   1354

6. What was the world population in 1960?

     a.   Around 4 billion

     b.   Around 3 billion

     c.   Around 2 billion

     d.   Around 1.5 billion

7. Under which dynasties was the Egyptian empire
     expanded between 1,570 and 1,200 BC?

     a.   Dynasty of XVIIIth

     b.   Dynasty of XIXth

     c.   Dynasty of XIV

     d.   Dynasty of XV

8. Around 1,500 BC, the great cities of which of the
     following civilizations were suddenly disintegrated?

     a.   Babylonian Empire

     b.   Assyrian Empire

     c.   Hittite Empire

     d.   Indus civilization

9. Most of the Zoroastrian areas came under the control of
     which of the following religions?

     a.   Islam

     b.   Shintoism

     c.   Judaism

d.   Hinduism

10. When was the former Han dynasty flourishing in
China?
a.   Between 102 BC and AD 109
b.   Between 2 BC and AD 299
c.   Between 202 BC and AD 9
d.   Between 302 BC and 9 BC

Answers Quiz 61

1.   (b) Between AD 661 and 750
2.   (c) Between 980 and 1015
3.   (a) 1402
4.   (b) Pegu (1369) or Bago
5.   (d) 1354
6.   (b) 3 billion
7.   (a) (b) Dynasties of XVIIIth XIXth
8.   (d) Indus civilization
9.   (a) Islam
10. (c) Between 202 BC and AD 9

Quiz No 62

1.   In America which empire collapsed suddenly in 1533?
a.   Aztec
b.   Olmec
c.   Inca
d.   Maya

2. In 1543, who arrived in Japan?
    a. Portuguese traders
    b. English traders
    c. Spanish traders
    d. Hungarian traders

3. In 1335, who was ruling most of India?
    a. Bahadur Shah Zafar
    b. Chandragupta Maurya
    c. Sultan Muhammad ibn Tughluq
    d. Rajaraja Narendra

4. When did Mongolia come under Chinese dominion?
    a. 1796
    b. 1496
    c. 1596
    d. 1696

5. When was Tula abandoned by Toltecs and there was a political fragmentation in Mesoamerica?
    a. 1475
    b. 1175
    c. 1375
    d. 1275

6. Between 1467 and 1477 where did the Onin Wars happen, and the country plunged into civil war?
    a. Iraq
    b. France
    c. Japan
    d. India

7. In the Subcontinent, when did Hindu Marathas begin to ravage southern regions, while some Rajput states and the Sikhs rebelled?

a. Around 1600

b. Around 1500

c. Around 1800

d. Around 1700

8. When was Fredrick I of Hohenstaufen ruler in Europe?

a. Between 1052 to 1090

b. Between 1352 to 1390

c. Between 1152 to 1190

d. Between 1252 to 1290

9. When did Roman emperor Constantine issue a declaration of toleration for all religions in the empire?

a. AD 313

b. AD 513

c. AD 413

d. AD 213

10. When was the Mycenaean palace system collapsed?

a. 1,000 BC

b. 1,200 BC

c. 1,400 BC

d. 1,300 BC

Answers Quiz 62

1. (c) Inca

2. (a) Portuguese traders

3. (c) Sultan Muhammad ibn Tughluq

4. (d) 1696

5. (b) 1175

6. (c) Japan

7. (d) Around 1700

8. (c) Between 1152 to 1190
9. (a) AD 313
10. (b) 1,200 BC

Quiz No 63

1. Where has the earliest modern-looking human (*Homo sapiens sapiens*) skulls yet found, that is about 130,000 years, old been found?
    a. Omo basin in Ethiopia
    b. Volta basin in Ghana
    c. Orange river basin in Lesotho
    d. Niger river basin in Mali

2. The earliest writings used to serve the purpose of registering religious traditions developed into which of these?
    a. Different languages
    b. Ancient legends
    c. Religious books
    d. Cave paintings

3. Where did the Olmec civilization emerge around 1,150 BC?
    a. Congo
    b. Australia
    c. Peru
    d. Mexico

4. Why was Mycenae in southern Greece named?
    a. After the treasury of Atreus
    b. After the fortress of Mycenae

    c.   After the tomb of Clytemnestra

    d.   After the Cyclopean walls

5. When did Ashoka, one of the most important rulers of Indian empire, convert to Buddhism?
- a. 465 BC
- b. 365 BC
- c. 265 BC
- d. 165 BC

6. When was the Chou dynasty flourishing in China?
- a. Between 1030 and 771 BC
- b. Between 830 and 571 BC
- c. Between 930 and 671 BC
- d. Between 1130 and 871 BC

7. When was Heraclius - from his reign the Roman Empire became an eastern Greek speaking state known as Byzantium - ruler of the Roman empire?
- a. Between AD 640 and 671
- b. Between AD 630 and 661
- c. Between AD 620 and 651
- d. Between AD 610 and 641

8. When did the Abbasid dynasty flourish?
- a. Between AD 950 and 1458
- b. Between AD 650 and 1158
- c. Between AD 850 and 1358
- d. Between AD 750 and 1258

9. When did the Mongols make their destructive conquests against the Sung China?
- a. Between 1671 and 1679
- b. Between 1571 and 1579
- c. Between 1271 and 1279

d.   Between 1471 and 1479

10. Which was a maritime empire that for centuries
controlled international trade passing through the straits
of Malacca and Sunda, and across the Isthmus of Kra?
    a.   Srivijaya
    b.   Heraclius
    c.   Theodora
    d.   Alexander the Great

Answers Quiz 63

1. (a) Omo basin in Ethiopia and Klasies River Mouth in
    southern Africa
2. (c) Religious books
3. (d) Mexico
4. (b) After the fortress of Mycenae in the eastern
    Peloponnese
5. (c) 265 BC
6. (a) Between 1030 and 771 BC
7. (d) Between AD 610 and 641
8. (d) Between AD 750 and 1258
9. (c) Between 1271 and 1279
10. (a) Srivijaya

Quiz No 64

1. When did the first anatomically modern human
    populations (*Homo sapiens sapiens*) begin to migrate
    northwards out of Africa?

a. Around 400,000 years ago
b. Around 300,000 years ago
c. Around 200,000 years ago
d. Around 100,000 years ago

2. What was the period of the Hammurabi empire, which was one of the early empires of Mesopotamia?
   a. Between 1,728 and 1,686 BC
   b. Between 1,828 and 1,786 BC
   c. Between 1,528 and 1,486 BC
   d. Between 1,628 and 1,586 BC

3. Where was the Gandhara state established in present-day Pakistan?
   a. South-eastern Pakistan
   b. South-western Pakistan
   c. North-western Pakistan
   d. North-eastern Pakistan

4. Throughout Eurasia, polytheism was the dominant form of religious belief before the first millennium. How was polytheism performed?
   a. All communities worshipping same god
   b. Individual communities worshipping their own gods
   c. Individual communities worshipping sun and fire
   d. All communities worshipping fire

5. Which of the following Roman emperors adopted the philosophy of stoicism in the face of adversity and wrote a book Meditations?
   a. Marcus Aurelius
   b. Antoninus Pius
   c. Vespasian

d.   Hadrian

6.   When did the T'ang dynasty establish in China?
a.   Between AD 418 and 707
b.   Between AD 718 and 1007
c.   Between AD 518 and 807
d.   Between AD 618 and 907

7.   When did Prophet Muhammad (PBUH) and his followers migrate from Mecca to Medina (the Hijra)?
a.   AD 722
b.   AD 622
c.   AD 422
d.   AD 522

8.   When was the Mali empire destroyed by Songhay?
a.   1746
b.   1546
c.   1646
d.   1446

9.   When did the Russians advance to the mouth of the Volga, gaining access to the Caspian?
a.   In the 1850s
b.   In the 1750s
c.   In the 1650s
d.   In the 1550s

10.   In 1389, which battle established Ottoman supremacy in the Balkans?
a.   Battle of Dimbos
b.   Battle of Zonchio
c.   Battle of Kosovo
d.   Battle of Ankara

Answers Quiz 64

1. (d) Around 100,000 years ago
2. (a) Between 1,728 and 1,686 BC
3. (c) North-western Pakistan
4. (b) Individual communities worshipping their own gods
5. (a) Marcus Aurelius (AD 161-180)
6. (d) Between AD 618 and 907
7. (b) AD 622
8. (b) 1546
9. (d) In the 1550s
10. (c) Battle of Kosovo

Quiz No 65

1. When did Vasco da Gama arrive in India?
    a. 1500
    b. 1494
    c. 1496
    d. 1498

2. When did the first agricultural settlement in South East Asia?
    a. 5000 BC
    b. 4000 BC
    c. 3000 BC
    d. 2000 BC

3. Which empire's rise happened in Africa in 1200?
    a. Mali
    b. Carthage

    c.   Songhai

    d.   Punt

4. Which of the following Byzantine emperors was the longest serving Byzantinian monarch with an effective reign from 976 to 1025?

    a.   Basil II

    b.   Jovian

    c.   Julian the Apostate

    d.   Arcadius

5. After the collapse of China's second dynasty, the Chou, which of the following dynasties did reunite China?

    a.   Tang

    b.   Han

    c.   Sui

    d.   Xia

6. Which of the following legends has been described in Homer's Iliad?

    a.   Atlantis

    b.   Exploding Lake

    c.   Trojan War

    d.   Oracle at Delphi

7. What is the period between AD 300 and 800 in Mesoamerica known as?

    a.   Early civilization

    b.   Classic world

    c.   Middle ages

    d.   Renaissance

8. The earliest root or tree crop cultivation - potatoes, yams, bananas - was characterized to which of the following regions of the world?

a. Oceanic
b. Antarctic
c. Arctic
d. Tropical

9. There have been eight Ice Ages in the last 800,000 years, alternating with warmer periods known as interglacials. How long were the interglacials?
   a. About 11,000 years
   b. About 12,000 years
   c. About 10,000 years
   d. About 8,000 years

10. When did Moscow and Vladimir fall to the Mongols?
   a. Between 1237 and 1238
   b. Between 1227 and 1238
   c. Between 1237 and 1248
   d. Between 1247 and 1258

Answers Quiz 65

1. (d) 1498
2. (c) 3000 BC
3. (a) Mali
4. (a) Basil II nicknamed as Bulgar-slayer
5. (b) Han dynasty
6. (c) Trojan War, Invasion of the city Troy by Mycenae empire in 1,250 BC
7. (b) Classic period or world
8. (d) Tropical regions
9. (c) About 10,000 years
10. (a) Between 1237 and 1238

Quiz No 66

1. During which of the following periods did the ice sheets advance across the frozen wastes of the northern hemisphere and temperatures fell by up to 15 degrees centigrade?
    a. Reconnaissance
    b. Prehistory
    c. Classical world
    d. Ice age

2. During which of the following periods did the rulers of Egypt construct a series of gigantic pyramid-tombs along the desert edge opposite Memphis?
    a. Late New Kingdom
    b. Middle Kingdom
    c. Old Kingdom
    d. New Kingdom

3. When were the first settlements established in Melanesia?
    a. Around 1,000 BC
    b. Around 4,000 BC
    c. Around 2,000 BC
    d. Around 3,000 BC

4. Under whose leadership Greeks formed an intimidating fleet and created an Aegean empire such as the cities of the Peloponnese?
    a. Hector
    b. Achilles
    c. Hercules
    d. Sparta

5. When was the Roman Republic government of Rome sacked?

  a. AD in 410
  b. AD in 455
  c. AD in 477
  d. AD in 487

6. When was Roman leader Justinian, who briefly recaptured western provinces but failed to reunite the empire, ruled the Roman empire?

  a. Between AD 527 and 565
  b. Between AD 507 and 545
  c. Between AD 547 and 585
  d. Between AD 557 and 595

7. The founder of which of the following religions was sent to prepare the Jews for the kingdom of God?

  a. Buddhism
  b. Taoism
  c. Confucianism
  d. Christianity

8. In Islamic World, when did one of the members of the ruling Umayyad family in Syria, Abdal Rehman I, seize power in Spain and made Cordoba his capital and resisted all attempts by the Abbasids to unseat him?

  a. AD 745
  b. AD 755
  c. AD 765
  d. AD 775

9. Before 1800, where did Portuguese establish colonies in Africa?

  a. Angola
  b. Algeria

c. Mauritania

d. Mozambique

10. When did Safavid emperor, Abbas the Great, die?

    a. 1649

    b. 1609

    c. 1629

    d. 1619

Answers Quiz 66

1. (d) Ice Age

2. (c) Old Kingdom (2685-2180 BC)

3. (c) Around 2,000 BC

4. (d) Sparta

5. (a) (b) AD in 410 and 455

6. (a) Between AD 527 and 565

7. (d) Christianity founder, Jesus of Nazareth

8. (b) AD 755

9. (a) (d) Angola and Mozambique

10. (c) 1629

Quiz No 67

1. When did the Aztec empire in Mexico fall to a force spearheaded by under 2,000 Europeans?

    a. Between1561 and 1566

    b. Between1544 and 1549

    c. Between1531 and 1535

    d. Between1519 and 1522

2. What were the Toungoo (1347), Ava (1364), and Pegu (1369)?

    a.   New political centres which replaced the old temple cities in Iran

    b.   New political centres which replaced the old temple cities in Turkey

    c.   New political centres which replaced the old temple cities in Burma

    d.   New political centres which replaced the old temple cities in Greece

3. Choose True or False: Most of the rivers in Russia follow a north-south axis?

    a.   True

    b.   False

    c.   None of the above

    d.   All of the above

4. When did missionaries of Cyril and Methodius make a voyage to Moravia?

    a.   AD 824

    b.   AD 884

    c.   AD 844

    d.   AD 864

5. Where can you visit a reclining Buddha from Polonnaruwa?

    a.   Sri Lanka

    b.   India

    c.   Afghanistan

    d.   Bhutan

6. Which of these had established an enormous empire in the subcontinent (undivided India) which stretched from Indus to Bay of Bengal by AD 400?
   a. Mughal empire
   b. Gupta dynasty
   c. Tughlaq empire
   d. Maurya empire

7. When was the period of 'Middle Kingdom' in Egypt?
   a. Between 3040 and 2783 BC
   b. Between 1040 and 783 BC
   c. Between 2040 and 1783 BC
   d. Between 83 and 40 BC

8. Which of these is a 14,000-year-old masterpiece and remains among the most potent and vivid images created by the artists of the late Ice Age in Europe?
   a. Bison from the caves at Altamira, Spain
   b. Horse from the Chauvet Cave, France
   c. Mammoth tusk sculpture, British museum
   d. Magdalian horse, France

9. When did bronze come into use in Southeast Asia?
   a. About 7,000 BC
   b. About 3,000 BC
   c. About 1,000 BC
   d. About 5,000 BC

10. When did the Ottomans defeat Persia and overran Syria, Egypt and Arabia?
    a. Between 1524 and 1527
    b. Between 1514 and 1517
    c. Between 1504 and 1507
    d. Between 1544 and 1547

Answers Quiz 67

1. (d) Between 1519 and 1522
2. (c) New political centres which replaced the old temple cities in Burma
3. (a) True
4. (d) AD 864
5. (a) Sri Lanka
6. (b) Gupta dynasty
7. (c) Between 2040 and 1783 BC
8. (a) Bison from the caves at Altamira, near Santander in northern Spain
9. (c) About 1,000 BC
10. (b) Between 1514 and 1517

Quiz No 68

1. During which of the following periods did the sea levels fall, opening up land bridges as so much of the Earth's water was locked into the sheets?
   a. Reconnaissance
   b. Enlightenment
   c. Ice Age
   d. Classical period

2. The first ruler of the Agade empire began his reign in 2,296 BC. What was his name?
   a. Manishtushu
   b. Rimush
   c. Naram-Sin
   d. Sargon

3. When was Mayan civilization destroyed?
   a. AD 750
   b. AD 850
   c. AD 1050
   d. AD 950

4. The first civilization of Europe was based on palaces furnished with colourful frescoes and provided with a sanitary and drainage system in the island of Crete. What is known as?
   a. Minoan
   b. Magdalenian
   c. Herculaneum
   d. Gothic

5. Around 1,200 BC which of the following religions appeared on the planet?
   a. Jainism
   b. Shintoism
   c. Zoroastrianism
   d. Islam

6. Which of the following nomadic groups broke through the Great Wall of China in AD 304 and within a decade sacked the capital of ancient Han dynasty, Chang-an?
   a. Hittite
   b. Hsiung-nu
   c. Assyrian
   d. Parthian

7. When did, for the first time, all of China lay under foreign rule?
   a. Under the Kublai Khan rule
   b. Under the Qin dynasty

    c.   Under the Hsiung-nu rule

    d.   Under the Han dynasty

8. Who conquered Lombard kingdom in 774?

    a.   Octavian Caesar

    b.   Louis XIV

    c.   Charles the Great

    d.   Peter the Great

9. When was Temujin proclaimed Genghis Khan 'universal ruler' of the Mongol tribes?

    a.   1260

    b.   1233

    c.   1236

    d.   1206

10. When did the Battle of Panipat happen in which Babur came out victorious and founded Mughal empire?

    a.   1526

    b.   1826

    c.   1726

    d.   1626

Answers Quiz 68

1. (c) Ice Age

2. (d) Sargon

3. (b) AD 850

4. (a) Minoan culture

5. (c) Zoroastrianism

6. (b) Hsiung-nu from Mongolia

7. (a) Under the Kublai Khan rule in the 1270s

8. (c) Charles the Great or Charlemagne

9. (d) 1206
10. (a) 1526

Quiz No 69

1. When did conquests of Chimu in central Andes begin?
    a. 1335
    b. 1355
    c. 1375
    d. 1365

2. In 1368 in China, who proclaimed himself the founder of a new imperial dynasty, the Ming, taking the title Hung-wu, meaning 'mighty martial'?
    a. Deng Xiaoping
    b. Mao Zedong
    c. Sun Yat-sen
    d. Chu Yuan-chang

3. Which ruler of Persia, with assistance from both Russia and the Christian West, managed to regain most of the lost territories from Sunnite Ottomans?
    a. Shah Abbas
    b. Reza Pahlavi
    c. Perdiccas
    d. Babak Khorramdin

4. The conquest of Sicily by whom in 1194 made the Hohenstaufen the richest rulers in Europe?
    a. Roger II
    b. Henry VI
    c. Roger I

d. Federick III

5. Who made a siege of Byzantinian Constantinople from 674-8 and then again in 717-18?
    a. Jews
    b. Hindus
    c. Muslims
    d. Christians

6. By the 3rd century AD, which of the following empires in China was ruling on a state that equalled the Roman Empire in population and stretched from the Pacific to the Taklamakan desert in central Asia?
    a. Han
    b. Shang
    c. Tang
    d. Sui

7. During which of the following centuries were principal preachers and reformers of Hinduism, Buddhism, Judaism, Confucianism and Taoism lived?
    a. In the 7th century BC
    b. In the 6th century BC
    c. In the 5th century BC
    d. In the 4th century BC

8. Buddhist images in Burma, Cambodia and Java date back …?
    a. Around AD 700
    b. Around AD 400
    c. Around AD 600
    d. Around AD 500

9. How were the Egyptian and Mesopotamian civilizations different from each other?

a. Mesopotamia irrigation system did rely on canals and dams as Egyptian due to the annual Nile flood

b. Egyptian irrigation system did rely on Tigris and Euphrates as Mesopotamia due to the annual Nile flood

c. Egyptian irrigation system did rely on Nile as Mesopotamia due to the annual Tigris and Euphrates flood

d. Egyptian irrigation system did rely on canals and dams as Mesopotamia due to the annual Nile flood

10. Beginning of the human population growth again after a period of stagnation?

a. 40,000 BC

b. 70,000 BC

c. 50,000 BC

d. 60,000 BC

Answers Quiz 69

1. (c) 1375
2. (d) Chu Yuan-chang (1328-1398)
3. (a) Shah Abbas
4. (b) Frederick's son Henry VI
5. (c) Muslims
6. (a) Han dynasty
7. (b) In the 6th century BC
8. (d) Around AD 500
9. (d) Egyptian irrigation system did rely on canals and dams as Mesopotamia due to the annual Nile flood
10. (c) 50,000 BC

Quiz No 70

1. The period 10,000 to 4000 BC witnessed which of the following critical developments?
   a. Origin of the settled life
   b. Origin of the first farming
   c. Origin of the first cities
   d. All of the above

2. When did the people of Olmec on the Gulf of Mexico, the Zapotec at Monte Alban and the Chavin in Peru establish the civilizations having a hierarchy of social classes, working civil service, efficient priesthood, and experts in manufacturing to commerce and government?
   a. Around 800 BC
   b. Around 200 BC
   c. Around 400 BC
   d. Around 600 BC

3. Who was the grandson of Chandragupta Maurya?
   a. Dasharatha
   b. Ashoka
   c. Maharaj Anant
   d. Narasimha Gupta

4. Who gained the control of Greece in the Battle of Chaeronea fought in 338 BC?
   a. Philip II
   b. Otto
   c. George II

  d. Constantine I

5. The first dynasty of China was flourishing from the 16th to the 11th century BC. Where was it established in China?
  a. Confederation of clans in the Xi River Valley
  b. Confederation of clans in the Mekong River Valley
  c. Confederation of clans in the Yellow River Valley
  d. Confederation of clans in the Yangtze River Valley

6. After AD 500, when nomads from the Asian steppes had sacked the narrow chain of empires extending from Rome to China, which of the following empires appeared in southeast Asia?
  a. Sri Vijaya
  b. Champa
  c. Khmer
  d. Majapahit

7. Which of the following prophets of God was born in the religious and commercial centre of Mecca?
  a. Mohammad
  b. Hud
  c. Saleh
  d. Noah

8. Who conquered England in 1066?
  a. Emperor Hadrian
  b. Oliver Cromwell
  c. William Tyndale
  d. William of Normandy

9. Between 1274 and 1281, who attempted to conquer Japan?
   a. Mongols
   b. Ottomans
   c. Abbasids
   d. Romans

10. Around 1300, which Turkish leader founded a state which became the core of the future Ottoman empire?
   a. Osman I
   b. Mehmed II
   c. Suleiman II
   d. Mehmed IV

Answers Quiz 70

1. (d) All of the above. The origins of the settled life; the first farming; and the first cities
2. (a) Around 800 BC
3. (b) Ashoka (273-232 BC)
4. (a) King Philip II
5. (c) Confederation of clans in the Yellow River Valley
6. (a) (d) Empires of Sri Vijaya and Majapahit
7. (a) Mohammad (PBUH)
8. (d) Duke William of Normandy
9. (a) Mongols
10. (a) Osman I

Quiz No 71

1. What is the origin of agriculture is often termed as?
   a. Mesolithic revolution
   b. Iron revolution
   c. Neolithic revolution
   d. Bronze revolution

2. Who established the Hittite empire between 1,344 and 1,322 BC?
   a. Arnuwanda I
   b. Suppiluliuma I
   c. Zidanta I
   d. Muwattali I

3. When was the first settlement established in New Zealand?
   a. About AD 850
   b. About AD 550
   c. About AD 650
   d. About AD 750

4. How many years did the Peloponnesian war last, in which Sparta fought against Athens?
   a. 29 years
   b. 23 years
   c. 25 years
   d. 27 years

5. The founder of which of the following religions was born in 486 BC?
   a. Islam
   b. Shintoism
   c. Buddhism
   d. Jainism

6. How can you find a connection between the Vandals, Suevi, Franks, Burgundians and the Alemanni?

    a. Large groups of Spanish tribes

    b. Large groups of Portuguese tribes

    c. Large groups of Hungarian tribes

    d. Large groups of Germanic tribes

7. When did the Othman rule Islamic civilization?

    a. Between 844 and 856

    b. Between 544 and 656

    c. Between 644 and 656

    d. Between 744 and 756

8. When did campaigns of Grand Prince Svyatoslav take place in Russia?

    a. From 964 to 971

    b. From 764 to 771

    c. From 864 to 871

    d. From 1064 to 1071

9. Where can you visit the Hindu-Buddhist kingdom of Champa?

    a. Along the coast of central Cambodia

    b. Along the coast of central Sri Lanka

    c. Along the coast of central India

    d. Along the coast of central Vietnam

10. Why did so many people in the valley of Mexico welcome the Spaniards in 1519?

    a. Because people have to pay heavy tributes to Tenochtitlan in food

    b. Because people have to pay heavy tributes to Tenochtitlan in textiles

c. Because people have to pay heavy tributes in increasingly in humans for ritual sacrifice to the Aztec gods (up to 50,000 year by 1510)

d. All of the above

Answers Quiz 71

1. (c) Neolithic revolution
2. (b) Suppiluliuma I
3. (d) About AD 750
4. (d) 27 years
5. (c) Buddhism, founder was Gautama Buddha
6. (d) Large groups of Germanic tribes
7. (c) Between 644 and 656
8. (a) From 964 to 971
9. (d) Along the coast of central Vietnam
10. (d) All of the above. Because people have to pay heavy tributes to Tenochtitlan in food, textiles and increasingly in humans for ritual sacrifice to the Aztec gods (up to 50,000 year by 1510)

Quiz No 72

1. The emergence of anatomically modern humans …?
    a. 200,000 BC
    b. 20 BC
    c. 2,000 BC
    d. 20,000 BC

2. What was difference between Mesopotamia and Egyptian dynasties?
   a. Egypt was more a territorial unit than the geographical concentration of cities in southern Mesopotamia
   b. There were almost no foreign invasions on Egypt contrary to Mesopotamia
   c. All of the above
   d. None of the above

3. When were the Marquesas islands first colonized?
   a. Around 350 BC
   b. Around 250 BC
   c. Around 50 BC
   d. Around 150 BC

4. Which of these were prime tragedy Greek playwrights?
   a. Aeschylus
   b. Sophocles
   c. Euripides
   d. All of the above

5. When was the ethical religion of Confucius spread in East Asia?
   a. In the 7th century BC
   b. In the 6th century BC
   c. In the 8th century BC
   d. In the 9th century BC

6. When did Chou replace the first dynasty of China, the Shang, and stretched to Yangtze valley as well?
   a. By 1327 BC
   b. By 1227 BC
   c. By 1027 BC
   d. By 1127 BC

7. When was the last time Constantinople sacked and Byzantine Empire collapsed for good?
  - a. 1553
  - b. 1253
  - c. 1353
  - d. 1453

8. When did Dutch East India Company establish Cape Colony?
  - a. 1352
  - b. 1452
  - c. 1652
  - d. 1552

9. How did the Europeans take advantage whenever Mughal or Safavid control faltered in India and Persia?
  - a. They served corporate entities
  - b. They served dacoits and thieves
  - c. They served princely states
  - d. They served feudal lords

10. Until which century, scarcely a decade passed without a recurrent plague outbreak in Europe?
  - a. Mid-18th century
  - b. Mid-17th century
  - c. Mid-19th century
  - d. Mid-20th century

Answers Quiz 72

1. (a) 200,000 BC
2. (c) All of the above

3. (d) Around 150 BC

4. (d) All of the above

5. (b) In the 6th century BC

6. (c) By 1027 BC

7. (d) 1453

8. (c) 1652

9. (a) They served corporate entities - the East India Companies

10. (b) Mid-17th century

Quiz No 73

1. When did the Maya civilization collapse?
   a. 550
   b. 650
   c. 750
   d. 850

2. Earliest Sanskrit writing in South-East Asia dates back to?
   a. Early 5ft century AD
   b. Early 2nd century AD
   c. Early 3rd century AD
   d. Early 4th century AD

3. When did the Mongol army reach the gates of Vienna while another defeated a German-Polish army at Liegnitz?
   a. 1241
   b. 1541
   c. 1441
   d. 1341

4. During the reign of which of the following rulers was Abbasid caliphate at its greatest extent?

    a.   Al-Mamun

    b.   Al-Masoor

    c.   Harun al-Rashid

    d.   Al-Qadir Billah

5. When did the Hsiung-un sack the ancient Chinese capital of Chang-an?

    a.   AD 416

    b.   AD 316

    c.   AD 116

    d.   AD 216

6. By exploiting quarrels with its neighbours, when had the Roman Republic emerged as the dominant power that controlled the whole of Italy and challenged Carthage, the other major power in the western Mediterranean?

    a.   By 64 BC

    b.   By 364 BC

    c.   By 264 BC

    d.   By 164 BC

7. Wheat and barley, sheep and goats were involved in the agriculture of which of the following regions from where it spread to Europe?

    a.   Central Asia

    b.   South Asia

    c.   West Asia

    d.   East Asia

8. Where was the imperial power of Huari, which flourished between AD 600 and 1,000, based?

a. Barberton Greenstone Belt

b. Peruvian Andes

c. Tibetan Himalayan

d. American Rockies

9. Who constructed the great pyramid in 2,590 BC?

a. Cheops

b. Shepseskare

c. Sahure

d. Neferure

10. The earliest cereal cultivation - wheat, rice, millet, barley was predominated to which of the following regions of the world?

a. Tropical

b. Semiarid

c. Temperate

d. Subarctic

Answers Quiz 73

1. (d) 850

2. (c) Early 3rd century AD

3. (a) 1241

4. (c) Harun al-Rashid (786-809)

5. (b) AD 316

6. (c) By 264 BC

7. (c) West Asia

8. (b) Peruvian Andes

9. (a) Cheops

10. (c) Temperate regions

Quiz No 74

1. When did the *Homo sapiens* migrate northwards from Africa?

    a.   100,000 BC

    b.   10,000 BC

    c.   1,000 BC

    d.   100 BC

2. How can you find a connection between early Sumerian settlement, the empire of Agade, III Ur empire and empire of Hammurabi?

    a.   Early empires of Europe

    b.   Early empires of Africa

    c.   Early empires of Americas

    d.   Early empires of Mesopotamia

3. When was Sub-Saharan Africa become separated by desert from the rest of the Old World?

    a.   About 200,000 years ago

    b.   About 100,000 years ago

    c.   About 10,000 years ago

    d.   About 1,000 years ago

4. When did the Persian empire collapse under the invasion of Alexander the Great?

    a.   31 BC

    b.   131 BC

    c.   231 BC

    d.   331 BC

5. When was the first dynasty of China established?

    a.   From the 11th to the 6th century BC

    b.   From the 14th to the 9th century BC

c. From the 16th to the 11th century BC

d. From the 15th to the 10th century BC

6. Missionaries sent by the Coptic church of Egypt in the 4th century spread Christianity in which of the following regions?
    a. Nubia
    b. Tunisia
    c. Botswana
    d. Ethiopia

7. When did Mongol invaders break the defenses of Russia?
    a. From 1267 to 1270
    b. From 1227 to 1230
    c. From 1237 to 1240
    d. From 1217 to 1220

8. Who developed new capital cities at Fatehpur Sikri and Isfahan?
    a. Darius the Great
    b. Alfred the Great
    c. Akbar the Great
    d. Abbas the Great

9. When did Chinese invasion of Mongolia end in the emperor's capture?
    a. 1249
    b. 1449
    c. 1349
    d. 1549

10. When did the Spaniards arrive in Mexico?
    a. 1519
    b. 1219

c. 1319
d. 1419

Answers Quiz 74

1. (a) 100,000 BC
2. (d) Early empires of Mesopotamia
3. (c) About 10,000 years ago
4. (d) 331 BC
5. (c) From the 16th to the 11th century BC
6. (a) (d) Nubia and Ethiopia
7. (c) From 1237 to 1240
8. (c) (d) Akbar the Great and Abbas the Great
9. (b) 1449
10. (a) 1519

Quiz No 75

1. When did the gradual changes in techniques of food acquisition over thousands of years until present day climatic conditions begin to prevail?
   a. Around 8,000 BC
   b. Around 5,000 BC
   c. Around 3,000 BC
   d. Around 1,000 BC

2. Why has the period between 1,200 and 900 BC been called a 'Dark Age'?
   a. Because 'Sea Peoples' attacked all the major powers of Eastern Mediterranean

      b.   Because 'Sea Peoples' overran everything

      c.   Because very few historical sources survive

      d.   All of the above

3. Lapita pottery is associated with which of the following people?

      a.   First inhabitants of Beringia

      b.   First inhabitants of Doggerland

      c.   First inhabitants of Melanesia

      d.   First inhabitants of Sundaland

4. When did the second civilization in Europe, Mycenae in southern Greece, emerge?

      a.   Around 1,500 BC

      b.   Around 1,800 BC

      c.   Around 1,400 BC

      d.   Around 1,300 BC

5. Which of the following religions thrived with the Indian empire of Ashoka?

      a.   Buddhism

      b.   Islam

      c.   Shintoism

      d.   Polytheism

6. When did Huns, nomadic tribes from Central Asia, defeat the Gupta empire of India?

      a.   AD 480

      b.   AD 580

      c.   AD 380

      d.   AD 280

7. Which of the following books conveyed the religion Islam to humankind?

      a.   Vedas

      b.   Agamas

      c.   Koran

      d.   Tipitaka

8. Until when did the German empire remain the largest in Europe?

      a.   1280

      b.   1270

      c.   1250

      d.   1260

9. In 1279, which of these completely occupied China?

      a.   Persians

      b.   Romans

      c.   Muslims

      d.   Mongols

10. When was there the introduction of iron and development of political elites in South-East Asia?

      a.   400 BC

      b.   500 BC

      c.   300 BC

      d.   200 BC

Answers Quiz 75

1. (a) Around 8,000 BC

2. (c) First inhabitants of Melanasian islands

3. (d) All of the above

4. (b) Around 1,800 BC two centuries later Minoan culture

5. (a) Buddhism

6. (b) AD 480

7. (c) Koran
8. (c) 1250
9. (d) Mongols
10. (b) 500 BC

Quiz No 76

1. Who built one of the Seven Wonders of the Ancient World, the Great Pyramid of Giza in Egypt?
   a. Neferkahor
   b. Nebra
   c. Djer
   d. Khufu

2. When was the Zapotec civilization emerged at Monte Alban, in Mexico?
   a. Around 1,749 BC
   b. Around 1,949 BC
   c. Around 1,849 BC
   d. Around 1,649 BC

3. Founder of which of the following religions was born in 486 BC?
   a. Polytheism
   b. Buddhism
   c. Shintoism
   d. Zoroastrianism

4. Which of the following is the world's oldest religion?
   a. Hinduism
   b. Islam
   c. Christianity

d. Buddhism

5. Which of the following wars were fought between 218 and 201 BC, in which Hannibal was defeated and Spain was annexed by the Roman empire?
   a. Third Punic War
   b. First Punic War
   c. Second Punic War
   d. First Crusade

6. After AD 500, whose invasions collapsed the narrow chain of empires stretching from Rome to China?
   a. Nomads from the South Asia
   b. Nomads from the Western Asia
   c. Nomads from the East Asia
   d. Nomads from the Asian steppes

7. Where did the Ottoman Turks first establish themselves and then conquered the Byzantium's European territories?
   a. Asia Minor
   b. South Asia
   c. East Asia
   d. Central Asia

8. Which of the following armies defeated Latin Christian, Byzantine, Persian, Indian and Chinese armies in a duration of one century?
   a. Jewish American armies
   b. Muslim Arab armies
   c. South Asian Hindu armies
   d. Southeast Asian Buddhist armies

9. When did the coronation of Otto 1 as emperor take place which sealed the connection between Germany and Italy?
   a. 1262
   b. 1162
   c. 962
   d. 1062

10. Where did the states of Kediri (12 century), Singhasari (13th century) and Majapahit (13 to 16th century) develop?
    a. North India
    b. West Indies
    c. Asia Minor
    d. Eastern Java

Answers Quiz 76

1. (d) Khufu or Cheops
2. (a) Around 1,749 BC
3. (b) Buddhism, founder Gautama Buddha
4. (a) Hinduism
5. (c) Second Punic War
6. (d) Nomads from the Asian steppes
7. (a) Asia Minor
8. (b) Muslim Arab armies after the death of Prophet Muhammad (PBUH)
9. (c) 962
10. (d) Eastern Java

Quiz No 77

1. When did the Inca empire in Peru fall to a force spearheaded by under 200 Europeans?
    a. Between1231 and 1233
    b. Between1331 and 1333
    c. Between1531 and 1533
    d. Between1431 and 1433

2. With the help of Medes, which Babylonian king re-captured the major Assyrian cities of Ashur and Nineveh?
    a. Hammurabi
    b. Marduk-zakir-shumi
    c. Marduk-nadin-ahhe
    d. Nabopolassar

3. When was the iron first brought into service in sub-Saharan Africa?
    a. Around 450 BC
    b. Around 550 BC
    c. Around 750 BC
    d. Around 650 BC

4. When did Alexander the Great invade the eastern Subcontinent?
    a. Between 329 and 325 BC
    b. Between 429 and 425 BC
    c. Between 229 and 225 BC
    d. Between 129 and 125 BC

5. Which of the following religions spread chiefly on account of the persecution of the Jews by more daunting neighbours?

a. Judaism
b. Jainism
c. Buddhism
d. Shintoism

6. Which of these was an envoy of the Han emperor who travelled between 138 and 126 BC?
a. Ibn Battuta
b. Chang Chien
c. Homer
d. Strabo

7. In which of the following centuries did the barbarian invade China?
a. In the 3rd and 4th centuries
b. In the 1st and 2th centuries
c. In the 5th and 6th centuries
d. In the 4th and 5th centuries

8. Who was ruler of Mercia from 757 to 796?
a. Offa
b. Wiglaf
c. Beorwulf
d. Eadwin

9. Who invaded Moscow and Vladimir between 1237 and 1238?
a. Ottomans
b. Mongols
c. Romans
d. Persians

10. When was the foundation of Pagan laid down in Burma?
a. 549

b.   649
c.   749
d.   849

Answers Quiz 77

1. (c) Between1531 and 1533
2. (b) Nabopolassar (626-605 BC)
3. (c) Around 750 BC
4. (a) Between 329 and 325 BC
5. (a) Judaism
6. (b) Chang Chien
7. (d) In the 4th and 5th centuries
8. (a) Offa
9. (b) Mongols
10. (d) 849

Quiz No 78

1. In Latin Christendom, which civilizations expanded faster than any 15th-century state?
   a.   Chavin
   b.   Moche
   c.   Aztec
   d.   Inca

2. The quickening in the pace of early human development stems largely on which of the following?
   a.   Beginning of agriculture
   b.   Beginning of garment making

c. Beginning of tool production

d. Beginning of leatherworking

3. When did Babylonian empire fall to the Persians?

   a. 739 BC

   b. 639 BC

   c. 439 BC

   d. 539 BC

4. When did iron come into use in sub-Saharan Africa?

   a. By 850 BC

   b. By 650 BC

   c. By 550 BC

   d. By 450 BC

5. With whom Greeks came into conflict within the central Mediterranean mainly over the control of Sicily?

   a. Carthaginians

   b. Valaginians

   c. Viraginians

   d. Anthropaphoginians

6. Which of the following Roman emperors was the author of Meditations?

   a. Hadrian

   b. Nerva

   c. Titus

   d. Marcus Aurelius

7. When is the martyrdom of Saint Peter and Saint Paul in Rome observed?

   a. August 29

   b. September 29

   c. June 29

d. July 29

8. After the birth of Prophet Muhammad (PBUH), for how long did Islam remain the western hemisphere's leading and most extensive civilization?
a. Almost 700 years
b. Almost 1,000 years
c. Almost 1,300 years
d. Almost 1,500 years

9. What were the Vikings known to the Slavs in Russia?
a. Collegians
b. Callipygians
c. Theologians
d. Varyagians

10. When did Timur or Tamerlane invade India and sacked Delhi?
a. 1398
b. 1698
c. 1598
d. 1498

Answers Quiz 78

1. (c) (d) Aztec and Inca
2. (a) Beginning of agriculture
3. (d) 539 BC
4. (c) By 550 BC
5. (a) Carthaginians
6. (d) Marcus Aurelius (AD 161-180)
7. (c) June 29
8. (b) Almost 1,000 years (One millennium)

9. (d) Varyagians
10. (a) 1398

Quiz No 79

1. In South America, who created a genuine imperial system, with a hereditary dynasty, and a highly trained bureaucracy?
   a. Maya empire
   b. Inca empire
   c. Olmec empire
   d. Aztec empire

2. In 1960, the world population was 3 billion. How many were the hunters and gatherers?
   a. 0.001 percent
   b. 0.0001 percent
   c. 0.1 percent
   d. 0.01 percent

3. What is the traditional date of unification of Egypt under Menes?
   a. 2,000 BC
   b. 1,000 BC
   c. 3,000 BC
   d. 4,000 BC

4. Which of these is a rock art painting that manifests two ancestral spirits of the Wardaman Aboriginal people from northwestern Australia?
   a. Alexander Mosaic
   b. Apollo of Veii

    c.   Severan Tondo

    d.   Lightning Brothers

5. When was King Philip II monarch of Greek empire whose well-trained Macedonian army declared war against Persia?

    a.   Between 59 and 36 BC

    b.   Between 159 and 136 BC

    c.   Between 359 and 336 BC

    d.   Between 259 and 236 BC

6. When did the Ostrogoths establish their control in Italy?

    a.   AD 493

    b.   AD 293

    c.   AD 193

    d.   AD 93

7. Which of the following nomadic tribes invaded and plundered Britain?

    a.   Kazakhs from Kazakhstan

    b.   Slavs from Slovakia

    c.   Picts from Scotland

    d.   Marauders from continental Europe

8. Until when did the relatives of Prophet Muhammad (PBUH) have political control over the Islamic empire?

    a.   AD 656

    b.   AD 660

    c.   AD 645

    d.   AD 650

9. In 212 BC, at the age of 75, who was killed by a Roman soldier?

    a.   Aristotle

b. Ptolemy

c. Pythagoras

d. Archimedes

10. When did Nadir Shah, who had usurped the Persian throne three years previously, invaded India and sacked Delhi, leaving the Mughal empire fatally weakened?

a. 1839

b. 1539

c. 1739

d. 1639

Answers Quiz 79

1. (b) Inca empire 'divine Incas'
2. (a) 0.001 percent
3. (c) 3,000 BC
4. (d) Lightning Brothers
5. (c) Between 359 and 336 BC
6. (a) AD 493
7. (c) (d) Picts from Scotland and marauders from continental Europe
8. (a) AD 656
9. (d) Archimedes
10. (c) 1739

Quiz No 80

1. The earliest millet and rice were grown in which of the following parts of the globe?

a. China

b. Middle East

c. Central Asia

d. South-East Asia

2. Who established a new political centre at Agade (also known as Akkad) with Akkadian replacing Sumerian as the main language of Mesopotamia?

a. Manishtushu

b. Sargon

c. Nanum

d. Shu Turul

3. When did the copper come into use in Europe?

a. Around 7,500 BC

b. Around 5,500 BC

c. Around 4,500 BC

d. Around 3,500 BC

4. What is the date of birth of Jesus Christ, the founder of Christianity?

a. 0 BC

b. 5 BC

c. 29 BC

d. 1 BC

5. When did Visigoths, a western confederation of nomadic groups, invade Italy and captured Rome?

a. AD 510

b. AD 210

c. AD 110

d. AD 410

6. Which of the following was the pivotal point that initiated the sequence of events that led to the First Crusade between 1096 and 1099?

    a. Victory of the Seljuk Turks over Byzantine

    b. Islamic recovery of Edessa

    c. Sack of Constantinople

    d. Rise of Salahuddin Ayubi

7. When did the Mongols complete the conquest of China?

    a. 1579

    b. 1479

    c. 1379

    d. 1279

8. When did Islam spread in Phillipines?

    a. In the 15th century

    b. In the 16th century

    c. In the 18th century

    d. In the 17th century

9. Under whose reign the Ottoman empire became of the world's largest powers and its capital, Istanbul, had become the largest city in Europe with 500,000 inhabitants?

    a. Mustafa Celebi

    b. Murad Sultan-i-Azam

    c. Suleiman the Magnificent

    d. Osman the Warrior

10. What was the name of Inca's son who extended the Inca empire to the north into Ecuador and south to Chile, and from the Pacific coast to the Upper Amazon?

    a. Yahuar Huacac

    b. Inca Roca

c. Capac Yupanqui

d. Topa

Answers Quiz 80

1. (a) (d) China and South-East Asia
2. (b) Sargon (2296-2240 BC)
3. (c) Around 4,500 BC
4. (b) 5 BC
5. (d) AD 410
6. (a) Crushing victory of the Seljuk Turks over Byzantine forces in 1071
7. (d) 1279
8. (b) In the 16th century
9. (c) Suleiman the Magnificent (1520-66)
10. (d) Topa

Quiz No 81

1. The earliest maize was grown as a staple crop in which of the following parts of the globe?
   a. Mesoamerica
   b. South America
   c. North America
   d. Carribean

2. When did the Persians end the Babylonian empire?
   a. 839 BC
   b. 739 BC
   c. 639 BC

d.   539 BC

3. In which part of the world, the inhabitants preferred the lifestyle of hunters and gatherers and acclimatized themselves to living in different environments from tropical forest to harsh desert?
    a.   Kalash in Asia
    b.   Saxons in Europe
    c.   Aborigines in Australia
    d.   Paleo-Indians in Americas

4. When did Mauryan Emperor Ashoka die?
    a.   32 BC
    b.   232 BC
    c.   132 BC
    d.   332 BC

5. Which of the following religions are known as the Great Missionary Religions because missionaries played a major role in spreading and linking the different areas?
    a.   Judaism
    b.   Hinduism
    c.   Buddhism
    d.   Christianity

6. When was the last Han emperor sacked?
    a.   AD 220
    b.   AD 120
    c.   AD 320
    d.   AD 420

7. The founder of which of the following religions claimed to be the Messiah or Saviour?
    a.   Christianity

b. Islam

c. Hinduism

d. Judaism

8. Which of the following dynasties ruled China after the Sui dynasty (581-617)?

    a. Yuan

    b. Tang

    c. Song

    d. Ming

9. After the conquest of which area in 1438, Inca control extended from Lake Titicaca to Huanaco in the north?

    a. Picchu

    b. Huayna

    c. Tupac

    d. Pachacuti

10. When did French peasant revolt (Jacquerie) take place?

    a. 1658

    b. 1558

    c. 1358

    d. 1458

Answers Quiz 81

1. (a) Mesoamerica

2. (d) 539 BC

3. (c) Aborigines in Australia

4. (b) 232 BC

5. (c) (d) Buddhism and Christianity

6. (a) AD 220

7. (a) Founder of Christianity, Jesus of Nazareth

8. (b) T'ang
9. (d) Pachacuti
10. (c) 1358

Quiz No 82

1. Animal-keeping dominated over plant cultivation in the steppe-lands of central Eurasia and domestication of which of the following animals facilitated a specialized lifestyle on nomadic herding?
   a. Wolf
   b. Horse
   c. Buffalo
   d. Goat

2. Under whose leadership Babylonian empire was ruled between 1,347 and 1,321 BC?
   a. Burnaburiash II
   b. Hammurabi
   c. Enlil Nadin Apli
   d. Tiglath Pileser

3. In which part of the Subcontinent had the Greeks and nomads established their empires after the death of Ashoka?
   a. South-east
   b. South-west
   c. North-west
   d. North-east

4. Which of the following conflicts happened between 431 and 404 BC?

a. Battle of Plataea
b. Battle of Cannae
c. Battle of Kalinga
d. Peloponnesian War

5. Which of the following was the capital city of the Han dynasty of China that had some 250,000 inhabitants?
   a. Chang'an
   b. Nanjing
   c. Luoyang
   d. Kaifeng

6. When did Prophet Muhammad (PBUH), founder of religion Islam, return to Mecca triumphantly?
   a. AD 130
   b. AD 230
   c. AD 330
   d. AD 630

7. When was the first Russian state, Kievan Russia, sacked?
   a. 193
   b. 1093
   c. 1293
   d. 93

8. When did the leader of a fanatical Shi'a Muslims, Ismail Safavi, reunify Persia, which was in a state of chaos since Timur's invasions?
   a. After 1200
   b. After 1600
   c. After 1500
   d. After 1100

9. Which nation occupied Annam between 1407 and 1427?
    a. Spain
    b. Britain
    c. China
    d. Portugal

10. In 1325, who arrived in the valley of Mexico and settled on a group of islands in the swampy margins of Lake Texcoco, where they built capital, Tenochtilan (site of Mexico City)?
    a. Totonacs
    b. Aztecs
    c. Puebloans
    d. Moches

Answers Quiz 82

1. (b) Horse
2. (a) Burnaburiash II
3. (c) North-west
4. (d) Peloponnesian War
5. (a) Chang'an or Xian
6. (d) AD 630
7. (b) 1093
8. (c) After 1500
9. (c) China
10. (b) Aztecs

Quiz No 83

1. Establishment of the earliest settled organised societies was made possible particularly after the introduction of which of these?
   a. Use of Iron
   b. Irrigation system
   c. Domestication of animals
   d. Cooking of food

2. Among the earliest civilizations, where was the ruler also the chief priest?
   a. Machu Picchu
   b. Harrah Pa
   c. Mohenjo-Daro
   d. Mesopotamia

3. People of which of the following civilizations abandoned most of the towns between 790 and around 860?
   a. Maya kingdoms
   b. Totonac kingdoms
   c. Teotihuacan kingdoms
   d. Puebloan kingdoms

4. Who was a popular invader of Gandhara state, present-day north-western Pakistan?
   a. Ashoka the Great
   b. Charlemagne
   c. Alexander the Great
   d. Genghis Khan

5. Which of the following cities is considered the birthplace of democracy?

a. Athens

b. Nippur

c. Memphis

d. Uruk

6. When did Augustus become emperor of the Roman empire?

a. 720 BC

b. 270 BC

c. 207 BC

d. 27 BC

7. In spite of suppression, discrimination and persecution, the communities of which of the following religions were established in several cities of the Roman empire by 200 AD?

a. Hinduism

b. Christianity

c. Islam

d. Judaism

8. In which of the following centuries were Muslim kingdoms invaded from the east, by the Mongols?

a. In the 11th century

b. In the 17th century

c. In the 13th century

d. In the 15th century

9. Which ruler extended the frontiers of the Mughal empire to Bengal in the east, to Gujrat and the river Godavari in the south, and to Kashmir in the north?

a. Aurangzeb Alimgir

b. Shah Jahan

c. Mohammad Shah Rangeela

d. Akbar the Great

10. When did the Union of Kalmar bring together Scandinavian kingdoms?
  - a. 1097
  - b. 1197
  - c. 1397
  - d. 1297

Answers Quiz 83

1. (b) Irrigation system
2. (d) Mesopotamia around 3,500 BC
3. (a) Maya kingdoms
4. (c) Alexander the Great
5. (a) Athens
6. (d) 27 BC
7. (b) Christianity
8. (c) In the 13th century
9. (d) Grandson of Babur, Akbar the Great
10. (c) 1397

Quiz No 84

1. When did Suleiman the Magnificent, son of Selim I, annex much of Hungary and besieged Vietnam, making the Ottoman empire one of the world's largest powers?
  - a. 1729
  - b. 1129
  - c. 1329
  - d. 1529

2. What are the small women statuette from the earliest farming villages of Catal Huyuk, Turkey called?

    a. Talaria

    b. Caryatid

    c. Terracotta figurine

    d. Venus figurine

3. Distinctive Lapita pottery sites are linked to whom?

    a. The earliest inhabitants of Polynesia

    b. The earliest inhabitants of Micronesia

    c. The earliest inhabitants of Indonesia

    d. The earliest inhabitants of Romanesia

4. Who was the father of Alexander the Great?

    a. Alexander IV

    b. Philip II

    c. Ptolemy I

    d. Philip III

5. When was the importance of Buddhism augmented and it expanded throughout India?

    a. After it was adopted by Mauryan emperor Ashoka

    b. After it was adopted by Persian emperor Darius I

    c. After it was adopted by Roman emperor Constantine the Great

    d. After it was adopted by Greek emperor Alexander the Great

6. When was the Gupta Empire collapsed?

    a. AD 910

    b. AD 710

    c. AD 410

d. AD 110

7. What is the migration of the followers of Prophet
    Muhammad (PBUH) to avoid the hostility of the
    merchants of Mecca in AD 622 known as?
    a. Imrich
    b. Hijra
    c. Mudo
    d. Ranne

8. In 732, in which battle Charles Martel defeated the
    Arabs?
    a. Battle of Cresson
    b. Battle of Harran
    c. Battle of Nicopolis
    d. Battle of Tours

9. Which Mongol emperor destroyed the Chagatai
    khanate, dislocated the Golden Horde, and defeated the
    Ottoman empire?
    a. Genghis
    b. Batu
    c. Timur
    d. Berke

10. When was the reign of Akbar the Great, which was the
    apogee of Mughal empire?
    a. Between 1156 and 1205
    b. Between 1256 and 1305
    c. Between 1556 and 1605
    d. Between 1456 and 1505

Answers Quiz 84

1. (d) 1529
2. (c) Terracotta figurines
3. (a) The earliest inhabitants of Polynesia
4. (b) King Philip II (359 - 336 BC)
5. (a) After it was adopted by Mauryan emperor Ashoka in 265 BC
6. (c) AD 410
7. (b) The hijra
8. (d) Battle of Tours
9. (c) Timur or Tamerlane
10. (c) Between 1556 and 1605

Quiz No 85

1. The damage to the structure of the Byzantine empire caused by which of the following crusades facilitated the Ottomans' rapid advance in the 14th century?
   a. First
   b. Second
   c. Fourth
   d. Seventh

2. Where has established cultivation of wheat and barley been confirmed around 7,000 BC?
   a. Anatolia to Zagros mountains
   b. Cape town to Baviaanskloof mountains
   c. Santiago to Andes mountains
   d. Queenstown to Remarkables mountains

3. What was the period of XVIIIth and XIXth dynasties when the Egyptian empire extended?
   a. Between 1,870 and 1,500 BC
   b. Between 1,170 and 800 BC
   c. Between 1,570 and 1,200 BC
   d. Between 1,370 and 1,000 BC

4. When did the Hindu religion, a Sanskrit literature, a caste system and iron working emerge in the Indus valley?
   a. Between 1,100 and 900 BC
   b. Between 1,000 and 300 BC
   c. Between 1,800 and 1,100 BC
   d. Between 1,500 and 800 BC

5. Which of the following Greek leaders led a successful campaign in India and Central Asia?
   a. Pericles
   b. Alexander the Great
   c. Leonidas
   d. Demosthenes

6. With shrines as far afield as northern Britain, which of the following religions was originated in Persia and spread widely in the Roman empire in the form of Mithraism?
   a. Hinduism
   b. Buddhism
   c. Jainism
   d. Zoroastrianism

7. Christianity was launched as a branch of Judaism, but when Jewish orthodoxy executed its founder, Jesus of Nazareth, its followers that converted to non-Jews came to be called as?

a.   Christians

b.   Muslims

c.   Zoroastrians

d.   Mithras

8. Which of the following dynasties was established in the Islamic World between AD 750 and 850?

a.   Early Abbasid Caliphate

b.   Early Umayyad Caliphate

c.   Early Seljuk Caliphate

d.   Early Mughal Caliphate

9. When did almost all of Africa remain independent of foreign control?

a.   1500

b.   1600

c.   1700

d.   1800

10. When did the Sunnite Ottomans under Selim I invaded Persia, and defeated Ismail Safavi at the battle Chaldiran and captured Tabriz?

a.   1814

b.   1714

c.   1614

d.   1514

Answers Quiz 85

1. (c) Fourth Crusade in 1204

2. (a) Anatolia to Zagros mountains

3. (c) Between 1,570 and 1,200 BC

4. (d) Between 1,500 and 800 BC

5. (b) Alexander the Great

6. (d) Zoroastrianism

7. (a) Christians

8. (a) Early Abbasid Caliphate

9. (d) 1800

10. (d) 1514

Quiz No 86

1. Which of the following was one of the most determining events of the world history?
   a. Smallpox pandemic
   b. Great depression
   c. Transformation from hunting and gathering to agriculture
   d. None of the above

2. Who controlled the greater part of Mexico and had entered Maya territory in Yucatan, when the Spaniards arrived in 1519?
   a. Cahokia
   b. Aztecs
   c. Norte Chico
   d. Puebloan

3. When did the Fourth Crusade take place?
   a. 1204
   b. 1096
   c. 1337
   d. 1453

4. Who attacked the Samarkand in 1219?

a. Charlemagne
b. Alexander the Great
c. Tamerlane
d. Genghis Khan

5. When was the mission of Augustine of Canterbury to England?

a. 397
b. 997
c. 597
d. 797

6. What do the Vandals, Alans, Suevi, Franks, Burgundians and the Alemanni share in common?

a. Nomadic tribes that invaded and plundered region of Western America
b. Nomadic tribes that invaded and plundered region of Western Europe
c. Nomadic tribes that invaded and plundered region of Western Asia
d. Nomadic tribes that invaded and plundered region of Western Africa

7. Who invaded and defeated the former Persian empire between 336 and 323 BC?

a. Ashoka the Great
b. Tamerlane
c. Alexander the Great
d. Attila the Hun

8. Where was the use of amber material begun in Europe?

a. Baltic
b. Eastern Europe
c. Western Europe
d. Southern Europe

9. Who ruled the Elam territory between 1,353 and 1,318 BC?

    a.   Mesanepada

    b.   Hammurabi

    c.   Tepti-ahar

    d.   Sagron

10. What do the first civilizations, Mesopotamia around 3,500 BC, Egypt around 3,200 BC, Harappa around 2,500 BC and China around 1,800 BC, share in common features?

    a.   City developments

    b.   Writing

    c.   Public buildings

    d.   Political system

    e.   All of the above

Answers Quiz 86

1. (c) Transformation from hunting and gathering to agriculture, from a migratory to a sedentary life

2. (b) Aztecs

3. (a) 1204

4. (d) Genghis Khan

5. (c) 597

6. (b) Nomadic tribes that invaded and plundered region of Western Europe, the Gual

7. (c) Alexander the Great of Macedon

8. (a) Baltic

9. (c) Tepti-ahar

10. (e) City developments, writing, public buildings and the political system

Quiz No 87

1. In 15,000 BC, the world population was 10 million. How many were the hunters and gatherers?
   a.   100 percent
   b.   80 percent
   c.   50 percent
   d.   10 percent

2. During whose reign was the rock-cut temple at Abu Simbel built?
   a.   Cleopatra VII
   b.   Khufu
   c.   Ramesses II
   d.   Djoser

3. Under which empire were the central Andes reunited in the 15th and 16th centuries?
   a.   Olmec
   b.   Inca
   c.   Teotihuacan
   d.   Pueblecon

4. Indian and Hellenistic traditions were intermingled in which of the following states established by Greeks?
   a.   Delphi
   b.   Corinth
   c.   Thebes
   d.   Kushan

5. When was Egypt invaded by Alexander the Great?

a. 338 BC
b. 336 BC
c. 332 BC
d. 330 BC

6. What do Judaism, Christianity, Buddhism, Hinduism, Taoism, Confucianism, Shintoism and Zoroastrianism share in common?
a. Religions that saw the rise in the 4th century
b. Religions that saw the rise in the 8th century
c. Religions that saw the rise in the 6th century
d. Religions that saw the rise in the 7th century

7. When was the fourth ecumenical council that tried to impose orthodoxy on the Christian world, the council of Chalcedon, held?
a. AD 551
b. AD 51
c. AD 251
d. AD 451

8. When did the Abu Bakr rule the Islamic civilization?
a. Between AD 132 and 134
b. Between AD 432 and 434
c. Between AD 532 and 534
d. Between AD 632 and 634

9. When did Emperor Frederick II die?
a. 1250
b. 1100
c. 1150
d. 1200

10. When was Nadir Shah assassinated and a period of anarchy started in Persia?

a. 1600
b. 1747
c. 1700
d. 1647

Answers Quiz 87

1. (a) 100 percent
2. (c) Ramesses II (1290-1224 BC)
3. (b) Inca
4. (d) Kushan empire
5. (c) 332 BC
6. (c) Religions that saw the rise in the 6th century
7. (d) AD 451
8. (d) Between AD 632 and 634
9. (a) 1250
10. (b) 1747

Quiz No 88

1. The evidence of foragers using sites year-round after the last Ice Age goes back?
    a. 10 BC
    b. 100 BC
    c. 10,000 BC
    d. 1,000 BC

2. When were royal tombs built in the Old Kingdom Egypt?
    a. Between 3,250 and 2,650 BC

b. Between 1,250 and 1,650 BC

c. Between 5,250 and 4,650 BC

d. Between 250 and 650 BC

3. Who ruled large parts of subcontinent between 273 and 232 BC and to develop a permanent reminder of his rule, inscribed edicts on pillars and rock-faces all over India?

a. Alexander the Great

b. Ashoka the Great

c. Akbar the Great

d. Peter the Great

4. When did Alexander the Great die?

a. 123 BC

b. 423 BC

c. 323 BC

d. 23 BC

5. In the Roman empire, who was Diocletian's successor that established a new capital at Byzantium in AD 330, Constantinople?

a. Caligula

b. Tiberius

c. Augustus

d. Constantine

6. Which of the following dynasties extended the Great Wall of China far to the north-west, fought against the nomad Hsiung-nu, annexed Vietnam and Korea, established authority over the Tarim basin and defeated the Min-Yueh kingdoms?

a. Han

b. Song

c. Tang

d. Xia

7. The meaning of which of the following religions are 'submission to the will of God'?
    a. Islam
    b. Hinduism
    c. Judaism
    d. Jainism

8. When did Muslims conquer Arabia and southern Palestine?
    a. Between AD 672 and 674
    b. Between AD 662 and 664
    c. Between AD 632 and 634
    d. Between AD 652 and 654

9. Where were the Mongols defeated in 1260?
    a. Caucasus
    b. Ain Jalut
    c. Gaza
    d. Yerusalem

10. Until when the Ottoman empire remained a formidable power, controlling the entire Arab world east of Libya and most of the Balkans?
    a. 15th century
    b. 13th century
    c. 16th century
    d. 19th century

Answers Quiz 88

1. (c) 10,000 BC

2. (a) Between 3,250 and 2,650 BC
3. (b) Grandson of Chandragupta Maurya, Ashoka the Great
4. (c) 323 BC
5. (d) Constantine
6. (a) Han
7. (a) Islam
8. (c) Between AD 632 and 634
9. (b) Ain Jalut
10. (d) 19th century

Quiz No 89

1. When did Columbus reach the Americas?
   a. 1480
   b. 1482
   c. 1496
   d. 1492

2. In the 7th millennia BC, where was sedentary farming begun?
   a. Kachi Plain of Pakistan
   b. Nile delta of Egypt
   c. Plain of North China by Hwang Ho
   d. East Anglia England

3. When was the imperial power of Huari in the Peruvian Andes flourished?
   a. Between AD 200 and 600
   b. Between AD 400 and 800
   c. Between AD 600 and 1,000
   d. Between AD 700 and 1,100

4. When was Mahavira, the founder of Jainism, born?

     a.   In the 8th century

     b.   In the 6th century

     c.   In the 2th century

     d.   In the 4th century

5. When were the Socrates tried and executed at Athens?

     a.   399 BC

     b.   379 BC

     c.   349 BC

     d.   359 BC

6. What is the date of birth of Gautama Buddha, the founder of Buddhism?

     a.   436 BC

     b.   446 BC

     c.   486 BC

     d.   426 BC

7. The founder of which of the following religions was executed as a revolutionary in AD 29?

     a.   Buddhism

     b.   Mithraism

     c.   Shintoism

     d.   Christianity

8. When did the coronation of Charles the Great or Charlemagne as emperor take place in Rome?

     a.   1,000

     b.   800

     c.   400

     d.   600

9. Mongol power crumbled in China with the rise of which civilization?
   a. Xia
   b. Qin
   c. Ming
   d. Han

10. When did Lithuania unite with Poland?
   a. 1346
   b. 1386
   c. 1316
   d. 1326

Answers Quiz 89

1. (d) 1492
2. (a) Kachi Plain of Pakistan in South Asia
3. (c) Between AD 600 and 1,000
4. (b) In the 6th century
5. (a) 399 BC
6. (c) 486 BC
7. (d) Founder of Christianity, Jesus of Nazareth
8. (b) 800
9. (c) Ming dynasty
10. (b) 1386

Quiz No 90

1. When was the rise of the Ottoman empire?
   a. Between 1501 and 1920

b. Between 901 and 1120

c. Between 1101 and 1320

d. Between 1301 and 1520

2. Animal husbandry and plant staples were the basis of the first economies which were mushroomed into which of the following regions of the world?

   a. North-East Asia

   b. North-West Asia

   c. South-West Asia

   d. South-East Asia

3. Under whose leadership Assyrian empire was expanded between 1,353 and 1,318 BC?

   a. Sennacherib

   b. Sargon II

   c. Ashur-Uballit I

   d. Tiglath-pileser III

4. Which of the following civilizations was the first to create a pictographic writing system that has not completely deciphered yet?

   a. Indus

   b. Mesopotamia

   c. Assyrian

   d. Hittite

5. Which of the following Greek leaders and his successors founded almost 70 cities making the Greek culture and language to spread as far as the borders of India?

   a. Achilles

   b. Alexander

   c. Hercules

   d. Hector

6. Seven states were competing for hegemony over China by 300 BC. When was it reduced to only one?

    a. By 290 BC

    b. By 21 BC

    c. By 221 BC

    d. By 121 BC

7. Which of the following Chinese dynasties stretched to its maximum in the 660s when 88 Asiatic peoples recognised Chinese overlordship, accepting its culture, its written language and its political institutions?

    a. T'ang dynasty between AD 818 and 1107

    b. T'ang dynasty between AD 218 and 507

    c. T'ang dynasty between AD 618 and 907

    d. T'ang dynasty between AD 318 and 607

8. Which of these was the period of most intensive Viking raids in Europe?

    a. Between 886 and 892

    b. Between 856 and 862

    c. Between 826 and 832

    d. Between 816 and 822

9. When was Mongol leader Timur born and died?

    a. Born in 1306, Died in 1415

    b. Born in 1396, Died in 1465

    c. Born in 1366, Died in 1425

    d. Born in 1336, Died in 1405

10. Who was Mughal emperor from 1627 to 1656?

    a. Shahjahan

    b. Aurangzeb

    c. Akbar

    d. Baber

Answers Quiz 90

1. (d) Between 1301 and 1520
2. (c) South-West Asia
3. (c) Ashur-Uballit I
4. (a) Indus civilization
5. (b) Alexander the Great (336-323 BC)
6. (c) By 221 BC
7. (c) T'ang dynasty between AD 618 and 907
8. (b) Between 856 and 862
9. (d) Born in 1336, Died in 1405
10. (a) Shahjahan

Quiz N0 91

1. When did Suleiman the Magnificent son Salim II manage to add Cyprus and Tunis in the Ottoman empire?
   a. 1570-2 and 1579
   b. 1570-1 and 1574
   c. 1570 and 1578
   d. 1570-4 and 1577

2. Where were the first Sheep domesticated around 9,000 BC?
   a. Mecca
   b. Medina
   c. Madurai
   d. Mesopotamia

3. What is the height of one of the Seven Wonders of the Ancient World, the Great Pyramid of Giza in Egypt?
   a. 170m (558ft)
   b. 120m (394ft)
   c. 160m (525ft)
   d. 140m (460ft)

4. By 800 BC, who had established complex settlements on the Gulf of Mexico with the population reaching up to tens of thousands?
   a. Olmecs
   b. Aztecs
   c. Incas
   d. Mayans

5. Which civilization ended in AD 700 in Mesoamerica?
   a. Pueblecon
   b. Chimor
   c. Teotihuacan
   d. Maya

6. When was the second Punic War fought, in which Hannibal was defeated and Spain became a province of the Roman empire?
   a. Between 298 and 271 BC
   b. Between 288 and 261 BC
   c. Between 218 and 201 BC
   d. Between 248 and 221 BC

7. When did White Huns invade Persia and kill the Sassanid emperor?
   a. AD 434
   b. AD 424
   c. AD 414

    d.   AD 484

8. How many are followers of Islam all over the world?
    a.   About 800 million
    b.   About 600 million
    c.   About 400 million
    d.   About 100 million

9. When did Frederick's son Henry VI invade Sicily which made the Hohenstaufen the richest rulers in Europe?
    a.   1194
    b.   1124
    c.   1294
    d.   1114

10. In 1603, who became the first Tokugawa shogun?
    a.   Tokugawa Ietsuna
    b.   Tokugawa Iemitsu
    c.   Tokugawa Hidetada
    d.   Tokugawa Leyasu

Answers Quiz 91

1. (b) 1570-1 and 1574
2. (d) Mesopotamia
3. (d) 140m (460ft)
4. (a) Olmecs
5. (c) Teotihuacan
6. (c) Between 218 and 201 BC
7. (d) AD 484
8. (b) About 600 million
9. (a) 1194

10. (d) Tokugawa Leyasu

Quiz No 92

1. When did Muslim seize power in Spain?
    a. AD 311
    b. AD 211
    c. AD 611
    d. AD 711

2. Where was the first cereal cultivated around 9,000 BC?
    a. Northern Palestine
    b. Northern Syria
    c. Northern Saudi Arabia
    d. Northern Turkey

3. Who was Sargon's grandson that expanded his empire further?
    a. Naram-Sin
    b. Shudurul
    c. Tutar-napshum
    d. Ibarum

4. By 800 BC, who had established complex societies in Peru with a population reaching up to tens of thousands?
    a. Norte Chico
    b. Toltec
    c. Chavin
    d. Moche

5. After the collapse of major cities of Indus valley civilization around 1,500 BC, which river valley by 600 BC had grown as the subcontinent's new centre of gravity?
    a. Brahmaputra
    b. Ganges
    c. Yarlung Tsangpo
    d. Padma

6. When was agriculture expanded to Britain and Scandinavia?
    a. Around 1,000 BC
    b. Around 2,000 BC
    c. Around 4,000 BC
    d. Around 3,000 BC

7. Which of the following religions thrived with the Persian empire of Cyrus and Darius the Great?
    a. Zoroastrianism
    b. Shintoism
    c. Buddhism
    d. Polytheism

8. By the 3rd century AD, which of the following empires was controlling an empire that extended between the Han empire on one end and Roman empire on the other end?
    a. Islamic world
    b. Persian empire
    c. Buddhist empire
    d. Maurya empire

9. When did Charlemagne conquer Lombard kingdom?
    a. 734
    b. 724

c. 714

d. 774

10. When was Timur's Turkish army destroyed by Byzantine empire at Ankara?

    a.   1102

    b.   1602

    c.   1002

    d.   1402

Answers Quiz 92

1. (d) AD 711
2. (b) Northern Syria
3. (a) Naram-Sin (2213-2176 BC)
4. (c) People in Chavin
5. (b) Ganges
6. (c) Around 4,000 BC
7. (a) Zoroastrianism
8. (b) Persian empire
9. (d) 774
10. (d) 1402

Quiz No 93

1. When was the second Ottoman siege of Vienna?

    a.   1613

    b.   1643

    c.   1633

    d.   1683

2. Ubaid period refers to which of the following?

    a.   Between 6,500 and 5,200 BC

    b.   Between 4,500 and 3,200 BC

    c.   Between 5,500 and 4,200 BC

    d.   Between 5,000 and 4,000 BC

3. When did the first king of the Agade empire, Sargon, start off of his rule?

    a.   2,396 BC

    b.   296 BC

    c.   2,196 BC

    d.   2,296 BC

4. When were the prime cities of Indus civilization fallen down?

    a.   About 1,000 BC

    b.   About 1,500 BC

    c.   About 2,500 BC

    d.   About 500 BC

5. When was the birth of Confucianism taken place?

    a.   551 BC

    b.   591 BC

    c.   511 BC

    d.   501 BC

6. When were the Trajan's Dacian wars fought?

    a.   AD 401 and 406

    b.   AD 301 and 306

    c.   AD 201 and 206

    d.   AD 101 and 106

7. When was the Sui dynasty established which reunified China after the barbarian invasions of the 4th and 5th centuries?
    a. Between AD 81 and 17
    b. Between AD 281 and 117
    c. Between AD 581 and 617
    d. Between AD 481 and 517

8. When did Constantinople fall under the onslaught of Turkish leader Mohammad II?
    a. 1483
    b. 1453
    c. 1423
    d. 1413

9. When did Genghis Khan attack the Samarkand?
    a. 1209
    b. 1219
    c. 1249
    d. 1299

10. Which of the following dynasties was established alongside the Sung dynasty?
    a. Tang
    b. Xia
    c. Qin
    d. Ming

Answers Quiz 93

1. (d) 1683
2. (c) Between 5,500 and 4,200 BC
3. (d) 2,296 BC

4. (b) About 1,500 BC
5. (a) 551 BC
6. (d) AD 101 and 106
7. (d) Between AD 581 and 617
8. (b) 1453
9. (b) 1219
10. (c) Qin or Chin dynasty

Quiz No 94

1. When was the first Ottoman siege of Vienna?
    a.   1599
    b.   1549
    c.   1529
    d.   1509

2. When were the first cereals cultivated in northern Syria?
    a.   Around 9000 BC
    b.   Around 5000 BC
    c.   Around 4000 BC
    d.   Around 2000 BC

3. When were the palace buildings at Abydos in Egypt developed?
    a.   1,100 BC
    b.   2,100 BC
    c.   100 BC
    d.   3,100 BC

4. Around AD 100, two remarkable pyramids of which of the following cities served to practice rites that included human sacrifice?

    a.   Cholula

    b.   Cusco

    c.   Pachuca

    d.   Teotihuacan

5. When were the first farming societies formed along the Danube valley?

    a.   Around 2,500 BC

    b.   Around 3,500 BC

    c.   Around 5,500 BC

    d.   Around 1,500 BC

6. Which of the following empires was stretched from the Atlantic to the Euphrates and from the English Channel to the Sahara?

    a.   Rome

    b.   Aztec

    c.   Mesopotamia

    d.   Maurya

7. The founder of which of the following religions was killed in AD 29?

    a.   Buddhism

    b.   Jainism

    c.   Mithraism

    d.   Christianity

8. When did the Umayyad Caliphate rule the Islamic civilization?

    a.   Between 691 and 850

    b.   Between 600 and 850

    c.   Between 661 and 750

d.   Between 611 and 710

9. Apart from Portuguese, which other European people
    established colonies in African before 1800?
    a.   British
    b.   Dutch
    c.   French
    d.   Hungarian

10. When was Sultan Muhammad ibn Tughluq ruling most
    of the India?
    a.   1395
    b.   1335
    c.   1385
    d.   1305

Answers Quiz 94

1. (c) 1529
2. (a) Around 9000 BC
3. (d) 3,100 BC
4. (d) Teotihuacan
5. (c) Around 5,500 BC
6. (a) Rome
7. (d) Founder of Christianity, Jesus of Nazareth
8. (c) Between 661 and 750
9. (b) Dutch
10. (b) 1335

Quiz No 95

1. When did Suleiman the Magnificent become Ottoman sultan?
   - a. 1550
   - b. 1500
   - c. 1420
   - d. 1520

2. How did the Neolithic people live on?
   - a. Domesticated animals and plants
   - b. Technological developments
   - c. Hunting and gathering
   - d. Nomadic way of life

3. When did inhabitants of Maya kingdoms abandon most of the towns?
   - a. Between 720 and 820
   - b. Between 710 and 810
   - c. Between 790 and 860
   - d. Between 700 and 800

4. Between 2,500 and 1,750 BC, which of the following civilizations were formed in the Indian Subcontinent?
   - a. Indus
   - b. Mughal
   - c. Maurya
   - d. Tughlaq

5. What did the Roman empire, that stretched from the Atlantic to the Euphrates and from the English Channel to the Sahara, originally consisted of?
   - a. A city-state governed by technocratic families leading an army of peasant soldiers

b. A city-state governed by aristocratic families leading an army of peasant soldiers

c. A city-state governed by bureaucratic families leading an army of peasant soldiers

d. A city-state governed by mobocratic families leading an army of peasant soldiers

6. Who adopted the title Shih Huang-ti (meaning the first emperor)?

    a. Shi Huang

    b. Emperor Taizu

    c. Emperor Wen

    d. Prince Cheng

7. When was the First Crusade fought?

    a. Between 1202 and 1204

    b. Between 1189 and 1192

    c. Between 1096 and 1099

    d. Between 1147 and 1149

8. When did Muslims occupy Bari in Europe?

    a. Between 841 and 871

    b. Between 831 and 891

    c. Between 821 and 861

    d. Between 811 and 851

9. After 1500, which leader of a fanatical sect of Shi'a Muslims reunified Persia, which was in a state of chaos since Timur's invasions?

    a. Zayd al-Balkhi

    b. An-Nasir

    c. Idris I

    d. Ismail Safavi

10. When was the writing in hieroglyphic script started off?

a. Around 7,000 BC
b. Around 3,000 BC
c. Around 5,000 BC
d. Around 1,000 BC

Answers Quiz 95

1. (d) 1520
2. (a) (b) Domesticated animals and plants and technological developments
3. (c) Between 790 and 860
4. (a) Indus civilization
5. (b) A city-state governed by aristocratic families leading an army of peasant soldiers
6. (d) Prince Cheng of Ch'in dynasty
7. (c) Between 1096 and 1099
8. (a) Between 841 and 871
9. (d) Ismail Safavi
10. (b) Around 3,000 BC

Quiz No 96

1. Who took the Constantinpole in 1453?
    a. Mustafa I
    b. Murad I
    c. Musa Celebi
    d. Sultan Mehmed II

2. When were the goats first domesticated around Anatolia and Zagros mountains?

a. About 2,000 BC
b. About 1,000 BC
c. About 7,000 BC
d. About 3,000 BC

3. When were the civilizations of Teotihuacan, classic Gulf coast, Zapotec, and Maya flourished in Mesoamerica?
   a. A classic period between AD 800 and 1200
   b. A classic period between AD 500 and 1000
   c. A classic period between AD 100 and 600
   d. A classic period between AD 300 and 800

4. When were the first farming societies formed along the Paris Basin?
   a. Around 4,750 BC
   b. Around 4,350 BC
   c. Around 4,250 BC
   d. Around 4,150 BC

5. During the 6th century BC, East Asia saw the rise of which of the following religions?
   a. Confucianism
   b. Polytheism
   c. Zoroastrianism
   d. Tao

6. When did the Sasanian Empire collapse?
   a. AD 361
   b. AD 61
   c. AD 161
   d. AD 261

7. Which of the following prophets of God was born around AD 570?

a. Sulayman
b. Mohammad
c. Ayub
d. Yusuf

8. When was Offa the king of Mercia?
   a. Between 777 and 826
   b. Between 727 and 756
   c. Between 757 and 796
   d. Between 707 and 746

9. When did the victorious commander of the Mongol forces in Europe, Ogedei, become successor of Genghis Khan?
   a. 1241
   b. 1641
   c. 1441
   d. 1041

10. What was the capital of the maritime empire of Srivijaya, which for centuries controlled international trade passing through the straits of Malacca and Sunda, and across the Isthmus of Kra?
   a. Phnom Penh
   b. Naypyidaw
   c. Manila
   d. Palembang

Answers Quiz 96

1. (d) Sultan Mehmed II
2. (c) About 7,000 BC
3. (d) A classic period between AD 300 and 800

4. (a) Around 4,750 BC

5. (a) (d) Confucianism and Tao

6. (d) AD 261

7. (b) Mohammad (PBUH)

8. (c) Between 757 and 796

9. (a) 1241

10. (d) Palembang

Quiz No 97

1. Where has the first domestication of goats been confirmed around 7,000 BC?

    a. Innsbruck to Nordkette mountains

    b. Anatolia to Zagros mountains

    c. Nagano to Hida mountains

    d. Denver to Rockies

2. When were pyramids built in the Old Kingdom Egypt?

    a. Between 2,950 and 1,500 BC

    b. Between 2,000 and 1,500 BC

    c. Between 1,650 and 1,000 BC

    d. Between 2,650 and 2,000 BC

3. Where in Europe did the first copper-working come into use around 4,500 BC?

    a. Balkans

    b. Scandinavia

    c. British Isles

    d. Eurasian Steppes

4. When were the inhabitants of North Africa become the earliest people to begin agriculture?

a. About 4,000 BC
b. About 10,000 BC
c. About 8,000 BC
d. About 2,000 BC

5. After the fall of western provinces of the Roman empire, how long was the East Roman empire, Byzantine empire, established?

    a. Almost 1,300 years
    b. Almost 700 years
    c. Almost 500 years
    d. Almost 1,000 years

6. When did the Roman army, with the help of Germanic tribes such as Franks and Visigoths, defeat the Huns ruler Attila at the battle of Chalons?

    a. AD 51
    b. AD 451
    c. AD 251
    d. AD 151

7. When was the Fourth Crusade fought after which the Byzantine empire disintegrated and Latin states were established all over the Balkans?

    a. 1096
    b. 1147
    c. 1204
    d. 1189

8. When did the Battle of Tertry take place in which Carlingians gain power in Francia?

    a. AD 887
    b. AD 187
    c. AD 87
    d. AD 687

9. When did Morrocan troop destroy Songhaai?

      a.   1191

      b.   1891

      c.   1591

      d.   1091

10. After 1500, which leader of a fanatical sect of Shi'a Muslims reunified Persia, and proclaimed himself Shah?

      a.   Hasan Ibn Ali

      b.   Ismail Safavi

      c.   Hussain Ibn Ali

      d.   Abu Abdullah Shia

Answers Quiz 97

1. (b) Anatolia to Zagros mountains
2. (d) Between 2,650 and 2,000 BC
3. (a) Balkans
4. (c) About 8,000 BC
5. (d) Almost 1,000 years
6. (b) AD 451
7. (c) 1204
8. (d) AD 687
9. (c) 1591
10. (b) Ismail Safavi

Quiz No 98

1. Capture of which land in 1354 was the first European foothold of the Ottoman empire?
   a. Ohrid
   b. Silistra
   c. Gallipoli
   d. Constanta

2. Established cultivation of wheat and barley is confirmed around?
   a. 2,000 BC
   b. 3,000 BC
   c. 7,000 BC
   d. 1,000 BC

3. When did the Suppiluliuma I establish the Hittite empire?
   a. Between 1,244 and 1,222 BC
   b. Between 1,144 and 1,122 BC
   c. Between 1,344 and 1,322 BC
   d. Between 1,300 and 1,300 BC

4. When was Gautama Buddha, the founder of Buddhism, born?
   a. In the 2nd century
   b. In the 8th century
   c. In the 6th century
   d. In the 1st century

5. Which of these great religions of the world originated in the same small region?
   a. Judaism
   b. Christianity
   c. Islam
   d. All of the above

6. Terracotta warriors were the army of which of the following?
   - a. Prince Cheng
   - b. Sun Yat-sen
   - c. Mao Zedong
   - d. Deng Xiaoping

7. After the death of Prophet Muhammad (PBUH) in AD 632 where did Islam spread the first?
   - a. Over the Hijaz
   - b. Much of central Arabia
   - c. Southern Arabia
   - d. All of the above

8. When did Rus attack on Constantinople?
   - a. 141
   - b. 341
   - c. 641
   - d. 941

9. Who was Akbar I or Akbar the Great?
   - a. Grandson of Babur
   - b. Third Mughal emperor in India
   - c. During his reign, Mughal empire tripled in size and wealth
   - d. All of the above

10. When was the Bronze Age in northeast Thailand and north Vietnam?
   - a. Between 2500 and 1500 BC
   - b. Between 1500 and 500 BC
   - c. Between 800 and 300 BC
   - d. Between 1000 and 100 BC

Answers Quiz 98

1. (c) Gallipoli
2. (c) 7,000 BC
3. (c) Between 1,344 and 1,322 BC
4. (c) In the 6th century
5. (d) All of the above
6. (a) Prince Cheng of Ch'in dynasty who took the title Shih Huang-ti (meaning the first emperor)
7. (d) All of the above, Over the Hijaz and much of central and southern Arabia
8. (d) 941
9. (d) All of the above
10. (b) Between 1500 and 500 BC

Quiz No 99

1. Who defeated Ottoman army at Ankara in 1402?
   a. Mongke Khan
   b. Ariq Boke
   c. Tamerlane
   d. Tolui Khan

2. Around AD 100, which of the following cities in Mesoamerica was designed in a precise grid plan and covered 8 sq miles (20 sq km) of the area with a population of some 200,000?
   a. Zuni Pueblo
   b. Teotihuacan
   c. La Isabela
   d. Iximche

3. When was the Gupta-Vakataka empire established in the Subcontinent?

    a.   Between AD 700 and 950

    b.   Between AD 100 and 450

    c.   Between AD 30 and 150

    d.   Between AD 300 and 550

4. What was the main reason for the spread of Judaism?

    a.   Persecution of Hindus by intimidating neighbours

    b.   Persecution of Christians by intimidating neighbours

    c.   Persecution of Jews by intimidating neighbours

    d.   Persecution of Mithras by intimidating neighbours

5. For Christianity, which of the following is the continent of its birth?

    a.   Europe

    b.   Asia

    c.   Africa

    d.   South America

6. When did Ali rule the Islamic civilization?

    a.   Between 656 and 661

    b.   Between 616 and 631

    c.   Between 626 and 631

    d.   Between 686 and 691

7. When did the emergence of Benin take place in Africa?

    a.   900

    b.   1000

    c.   1300

d.   1600

8.   In 1526, Who defeated the last of the Sultans of Delhi
at Panipat?
a.   Babur
b.   Rangeela
c.   Akbar
d.   Aurangzeb

9.   When was the last Safavid shah overthrown by Afghan
rebels?
a.   1422
b.   1722
c.   1022
d.   1222

10.   Who assumed power in 1603 in Japan and established
the dynasty of shoguns who ruled Japan until the 19th
century?
a.   Tokugawa Iemochi
b.   Tokugawa Iesada
c.   Tokugawa Ienobu
d.   Tokugawa Ieyasu

Answers Quiz 99

1.   (c) Tamerlane or Timur
2.   (b) Teotihuacan
3.   (d) Between AD 300 and 550
4.   (c) Persecution of Jews by intimidating neighbours
5.   (b) Asia
6.   (a) Between 656 and 661
7.   (c) 1300

8. (a) Babur - a descendant of Timur

9. (b) 1722

10. (d) Tokugawa Ieyasu

Quiz No 100

1. When did the accession of Gallipoli take place with Ottoman empire?
   a. 1654
   b. 1354
   c. 954
   d. 1054

2. How were the Neolithic settlements expanded to Mesopotamian plains between 6,000 and 5,000 BC?
   a. Due to the development of road systems
   b. Due to the development of castle systems
   c. Due to the development of agricultural systems
   d. Due to the development of irrigation systems

3. When was the Mittani territory stretched to its best limit?
   a. Between 1,280 and 1,040 BC
   b. Between 1,080 and 740 BC
   c. Between 1,880 and 1,040 BC
   d. Between 1,480 and 1,340 BC

4. When was the earliest settlement established in Australia from southeast Asia?
   a. Around 50,000 BC
   b. Around 5,000 BC

c. Around 500 BC

d. Around 50 BC

5. Evidence of the earliest Sanskrit writing in Southeast Asia goes back?

    a. To the 1st century AD

    b. To the 5th century AD

    c. To the 3rd century AD

    d. To the 7th century AD

6. Ashoka was one of the most distinguished rulers of which of the following empires?

    a. Persian

    b. Indian

    c. Roman

    d. Ottoman

7. When did Prophet Muhammad (PBUH) die?

    a. AD 332

    b. AD 632

    c. AD 232

    d. AD 32

8. When did the Battle of Tagliacozzo happen?

    a. 868

    b. 1468

    c. 1068

    d. 1268

9. In 1591, Moroccan troops destroyed which of the following civilizations?

    a. Songhai

    b. Berber

    c. Saadi

    d. Alouite

10. Who was Timur or Tamerlane?

    a.   A descendant of Gautam Buddha

    b.   A descendant of Alexander the Great

    c.   A descendant of Genghis Khan

    d.   A descendant of Ashoka the Great

Answers Quiz 100

1. (b) 1354

2. (d) Due to the development of irrigation systems

3. (d) Between 1,480 and 1,340 BC

4. (a) Around 50,000 BC

5. (c) To the 3rd century AD

6. (b) Indian

7. (b) AD 632

8. (d) 1268

9. (a) Songhai empire

10. (c) A descendant of Genghis Khan

Quiz No 101

1. Pre-pottery Neolithic period refers to which of these?

    a.   Between 900 and 500 BC

    b.   Between 9,000 and 6,500 BC

    c.   Between 5,000 and 1,500 BC

    d.   Between 10,000 and 8,500 BC

2. When did Hammurabi initiate his rule?

    a.   1,528 BC

      b.   1,328 BC

      c.   1,128 BC

      d.   1,728 BC

3. When did the first camels arrive in Africa from Asia?

      a.   Around 1,000 BC

      b.   Around 100 BC

      c.   Around 1 BC

      d.   Around 10 BC

4. During the Classic period which of the following countries in Europe was divided into city-states?

      a.   Russia

      b.   Germany

      c.   Greece

      d.   Norway

5. When was the last western Roman emperor deposed?

      a.   AD 776

      b.   AD 876

      c.   AD 476

      d.   AD 76

6. Which of the following books was revealed by God to Muhammad his prophet?

      a.   Koran

      b.   Torah

      c.   Zabur

      d.   Injil

7. Between 856 and 862, whose raids were most intensive in Europe?

      a.   Vikings

      b.   Mongols

      c.   Muslims

d. Magyars

8. Which of these was a descendant of Timur or
Tamerlane and first Mughal emperor?
   a. Akbar
   b. Aurangzeb
   c. Rangeela
   d. Babur

9. In the early 15th century, a series of voyages of which
Muslim admiral all over the South-East Asia, revived
and reinforced China's system of tributary
relationships?
   a. Ibn Batuta
   b. Cheng Ho
   c. Vasco de Gama
   d. Al-Masudi

10. When did the accession of Osman take place with
Ottoman empire?
   a. 1581
   b. 1081
   c. 1281
   d. 1181

Answers Quiz 101

1. (b) Between 9,000 and 6,500 BC
2. (d) 1,728 BC
3. (b) Around 100 BC
4. (c) Greece
5. (c) AD 476
6. (a) Koran

7. (a) Vikings

8. (d) Zahir uddin Babur

9. (b) Muslim admiral Cheng Ho

10. (c) 1281

Quiz No 102

1. When did in China the urban civilization arise?
   a. By 1,800
   b. By 1,200
   c. By 1,000
   d. By 1,400

2. Who was the last pharaoh of Egypt?
   a. Amenhotep III
   b. Thutmose III
   c. Tutankhamun
   d. Rameses III

3. The war reduced the 16 political units of the subcontinent's new centre of gravity, Ganges, to how many units by 400 BC?
   a. 4
   b. 6
   c. 8
   d. 2

4. What is the date of birth and death of Confucius, the founder of the ethical religion of Confucianism which spread in the 6th century in East Asia?
   a. Between 581 and 499 BC
   b. Between 551 and 479 BC

     c.   Between 521 and 439 BC

     d.   Between 511 and 429 BC

5. During the 3rd, 4th and 5th centuries AD, which of the following were expert horsemen who possessed in war a speed and striking power that their opponents could rarely match?

     a.   Magyars

     b.   Romans

     c.   Nomadic tribes

     d.   Persians

6. When did the Sung dynasty establish in China?

     a.   Between AD 660 and 1079

     b.   Between AD 460 and 979

     c.   Between AD 960 and 1279

     d.   Between AD 160 and 579

7. When did the Fatimids dynasty capture Cairo?

     a.   AD 969

     b.   AD 669

     c.   AD 369

     d.   AD 69

8. When did Vikings seize Novgorod in Russia?

     a.   1862

     b.   662

     c.   862

     d.   82

9. In 1258, which of these destroyed Baghdad?

     a.   Mongols

     b.   Vikings

     c.   Romans

     d.   Persians

10. When did Constantinople fall at the hands of the leader of Ottoman army Sultan Mehmet II?
    a. 09 May 1451
    b. 09 May 1453
    c. 29 May 1453
    d. 29 May 1451

Answers Quiz 102

1. (a) By 1,800
2. (d) Rameses III
3. (a) 4
4. (b) Between 551 and 479 BC
5. (c) Nomadic tribes
6. (c) Between AD 960 and 1279
7. (a) AD 969
8. (c) 862
9. (a) Mongols
10. (c) 29 May 1453

Quiz No 103

1. Pottery Neolithic period refers to which of these?
    a. Between 7,000 and 6,000 BC
    b. Between 7,500 and 6,500 BC
    c. Between 6,000 and 5,000 BC
    d. Between 6,500 and 5,500 BC

2. Astronomy and astrology experts of which of the following civilizations were the first to calculate the exact length of the solar year and the lunar month and guessed eclipses?

    a.   Indus

    b.   Mayan

    c.   Mesopotamia

    d.   Egyptian

3. Under whose reign Gandhara region was converted to Buddhism?

    a.   Mohammd Shah Rangeela

    b.   Zahir uddin Babar

    c.   Ashoka the Great

    d.   Akbar the Great

4. Originated in Persia, which of the following religions presented life as a battleground between the forces of good and evil?

    a.   Zoroastrianism

    b.   Judaism

    c.   Shintoism

    d.   Buddhism

5. When was the last Han emperor abdicated?

    a.   AD 20

    b.   AD 420

    c.   AD 220

    d.   AD 120

6. Which of the following made popular missionary journeys between AD 46 and 57?

    a.   St Boniface

    b.   St Paul

    c.   St Barnabas

      d.   Augustine of Canterbury

7. Who was the cousin and son-in-law of the Prophet Muhammad (PBUH)?
      a.   Umar
      b.   Abu Bakr
      c.   Ali
      d.   Usman

8. Why is the year AD 632 important in Islamic history?
      a.   Karbala
      b.   Al Hijra
      c.   Death of Muhammad
      d.   Umar became Caliph

9. When did Portuguese destroy the Mwenemutapa empire in Africa?
      a.   1528
      b.   1628
      c.   1601
      d.   1690

10. During the civil war from 1467 to 1590, Daimyo clans had the most powerful influence in which county?
      a.   Japan
      b.   Iran
      c.   Pakistan
      d.   Australia

Answers Quiz 103

1.   (d) Between 6,500 and 5,500 BC
2.   (b) Maya kingdoms

3. (c) Ashoka the Great (273-232 BC)

4. (a) Zoroastrianism

5. (c) AD 220

6. (b) St Paul

7. (c) Ali Ibn Talib

8. (c) Death of Prophet Muhammad (PBUH)

9. (b) 1628

10. (a) Japan

Quiz No 104

1. When was the rise of the Ottoman empire at its highest?

    a. Between 801 and 1120

    b. Between 1101 and 1320

    c. Between 1301 and 1520

    d. Between 1701 and 1920

2. Uruk period refers to which of the following?

    a. Between 200 and 100 BC

    b. Between 4,200 and 3,100 BC

    c. Between 1,200 and 1,100 BC

    d. Between 3,200 and 2,100 BC

3. When did the Olmec civilization emerge in Mexico?

    a. Around 50 BC

    b. Around 1,500 BC

    c. Around 150 BC

    d. Around 1,150 BC

4. When was the first civilization of Europe, which was based on palaces furnished with colourful frescoes and provided with a sanitary and drainage system in the island of Crete, established?

    a.   About 5,000 BC

    b.   About 500 BC

    c.   About 2,000 BC

    d.   About 1,000 BC

5. Which of the following empires collapsed in a series of civil wars?

    a.   Roman Republic

    b.   Anasazi

    c.   Cahokia

    d.   Easter Island

6. After AD 500, when nomads from the Asian steppes had sacked the narrow chain of empires extending from Rome to China which of the following civilizations emerged in America?

    a.   Maya

    b.   Aztec

    c.   Inca

    d.   All of the above

7. In 687, in which battle Carlingians gained power in Francia?

    a.   Battle of Tertry

    b.   Battle of Lepanto

    c.   Battle of Adrianople

    d.   Battle of Milvian Bridge

8. When did the civil war in Japan take place?

    a.   Between 1437 and 1599

    b.   Between 1427 and 1550

    c.   Between 1407 and 1500

    d.   Between 1467 and 1590

9. In which year was the foundation of the Delhi Sultanate laid down?

    a. 1196
    b. 1186
    c. 1216
    d. 1206

10. In 1652, who established Cape Colony?

    a. Dutch
    b. British
    c. French
    d. Danish

Answers Quiz 104

1. (c) Between 1301 and 1520
2. (b) Between 4,200 and 3,100 BC
3. (d) Around 1,150 BC
4. (c) About 2,000 BC
5. (a) Roman Republic
6. (d) All of the above, The Maya, Aztec and Inca
7. (a) Battle of Tertry
8. (d) Between 1467 and 1590
9. (d) 1206
10. (a) Dutch

Quiz No 105

1. What is the date of the first cereal cultivation in Syria?

      a.   2,000 BC

      b.   9,000 BC

      c.   3,000 BC

      d.   5,000 BC

2. When were towns and cities built in the Old Kingdom Egypt?

      a.   Between 250 and 20 BC

      b.   Between 4,250 and 1,000 BC

      c.   Between 1,250 and 1,000 BC

      d.   Between 3,250 and 2,000 BC

3. When was Teotihuacan civilization collapsed?

      a.   AD 200

      b.   AD 700

      c.   AD 500

      d.   AD 900

4. When was Troy invaded by Mycenaeans?

      a.   1,750 BC

      b.   1,550 BC

      c.   1,250 BC

      d.   1,050 BC

5. When was the Edict of Milan, in which tolerance was proclaimed for all religions in the Roman empire, signed?

      a.   AD 113

      b.   AD 313

      c.   AD 513

      d.   AD 13

6. What do the Avars, Slavs, and the Bulgars share in common?

      a.   Nomadic tribes who ravaged the Balkans

b. Nomadic tribes who ravaged the Caucasus

c. Nomadic tribes who ravaged the British Isles

d. Nomadic tribes who ravaged the Scandinavia

7. In which of the following centuries were Muslim kingdoms invaded from the west, the Crusades?

a. In the 14th century

b. In the 12th century

c. In the 16th century

d. In the 10th century

8. The Late Classic (600-900 AD) and the Terminal Classic (850-1050 AD) were the periods of which civilization's history?

a. Mayan

b. Islamic

c. Cahokian

d. Roman

9. Who was the founder of the Ming dynasty?

a. Liu Bang

b. Chu Yuan-chang

c. Wang Mang

d. Ying Zheng

10. With the decline of Srivijaya civilization, when did a powerful new Muslim state emerged at Malaca?

a. After 1000

b. After 1300

c. After 1400

d. After 1800

Answers Quiz 105

1. (b) 9,000 BC
2. (d) Between 3,250 and 2,000 BC
3. (b) AD 700
4. (c) 1,250 BC
5. (b) AD 313
6. (a) Nomadic tribes who ravaged the Balkans
7. (b) In the 12th century
8. (a) The Mayan civilization
9. (b) Chu Yuan-chang (1328-98)
10. (c) After 1400

Quiz No 106

1. What is the date of the Neolithic period in China?
    a. Between 3,500 and 500 BC
    b. Between 5,500 and 2,500 BC
    c. Between 9,500 and 5,500 BC
    d. Between 7,500 and 3,500 BC

2. The king of Yaxchilan belonged to which of the following civilizations?
    a. Cahokia
    b. Maya
    c. Inca
    d. Indus

3. When did bronze-working arise in Southeast Asia?
    a. Around 500 BC
    b. Around 700 BC

c. Around 100 BC

d. Around 1,000 BC

4. When was the centrepiece of Athens, Parthenian, begun?

    a. 247 BC

    b. 147 BC

    c. 447 BC

    d. 47 BC

5. When was Prince Cheng of Ch'in who adopted the title of Shih Huang-ti became the first emperor of China?

    a. 221 BC

    b. 321 BC

    c. 521 BC

    d. 21 BC

6. Which of the following ecumenical councils isolated the Monophysites and Nestorians?

    a. First ecumenical council

    b. Second ecumenical council

    c. Third ecumenical council

    d. Fourth ecumenical council

7. Which of the following dynasties was established in the Islamic World between AD 661 and 750?

    a. Abbasid Caliphate

    b. Umayyad Caliphate

    c. Ottoman Sultanate

    d. Rashidun Caliphate

8. When did Portuguese establish trading posts in east Africa?

    a. 1705

    b. 1205

c. 1505

d. 1105

9. When did Turkish leader Mohammad II reign under which the fate of Byzantine empire was sealed?
    a. Between 1651 and 1681
    b. Between 1251 and 1281
    c. Between 1151 and 1181
    d. Between 1451 and 1481

10. When did rebellion of Florentine clothworkers (ciompi) take place?
    a. 1578
    b. 1278
    c. 1378
    d. 1178

Answers Quiz 106

1. (d) Between 7,500 and 3,500 BC
2. (b) Maya kingdoms
3. (d) Around 1,000 BC
4. (c) 447 BC
5. (a) 221 BC
6. (a) The fourth ecumenical council, council of Chalcedon held in AD 451
7. (b) Umayyad Caliphate
8. (c) 1505
9. (b) Between 1451 and 1481
10. (c) 1378

Quiz No 107

1. What is the date of the first rice cultivation in South Asia?
    a. 5,000 BC
    b. 7,000 BC
    c. 9,000 BC
    d. 10,000 BC

2. When were the central Andes reunited under Inca civilization?
    a. In the 15th century
    b. In the 16th century
    c. In the 17th century
    d. In the 18th century

3. Which civilization in Europe created a script known as Linear B, which was an early version of Greek?
    a. Dorian
    b. Hittite
    c. Illyrian
    d. Mycenae

4. Which of the following defeated western provinces of Roman Republic in the early 5th century?
    a. Muslims invaders
    b. Viking invaders
    c. Germanic invaders
    d. Magyar invaders

5. Which of the following nomadic tribes invaded the Gaul region of Western Europe in AD 406?
    a. Vandals
    b. Alans

c. Suevi

d. All of the above

6. When did Omar rule the Islamic civilization?

    a. Between 656 and 661

    b. Between 644 and 656

    c. Between 634 and 644

    d. Between 632 and 634

7. When did Alexander of Novgorod defeat Swedes at the River Neva?

    a. 1340

    b. 1200

    c. 1240

    d. 1140

8. Who invaded Poland and Hungary in 1241?

    a. Mongols

    b. Ottomans

    c. Germanics

    d. Magyars

9. In Vietnam, which new kingdom emerged which gradually absorbed Champa by annexing its capital, Vijaya in 1471?

    a. Hong Bang

    b. Dai Viet

    c. Thuc

    d. Trung

10. In their time, who ruled large stretches of territory in what is now southern Mexico, Guatemala, Belize, Honduras?

    a. Cahokians

    b. Teotihuacans

c. Mayans
d. Olmecs

Answers Quiz 107

1. (b) 7,000 BC
2. (a) (b) In the 15th and 16th centuries
3. (d) Mycenae in southern Greece
4. (c) Germanic invaders
5. (d) The Vandals, Alans and Suevi
6. (c) Between 634 and 644
7. (c) 1240
8. (a) Mongols
9. (b) Dai Viet
10. (c) Mayans

Quiz No 108

1. When was the Inca empire at its peak?
   a. Between 250 and 900
   b. Between 1600 and 300 BC
   c. Between 1050 and 1205
   d. Between 1438 and 1525

2. Where were cities persisted around 3,500 BC?
   a. Mesopotamia
   b. Balkans
   c. Middle East
   d. South Africa

3. Where did the Zapotec civilization emerge around 1,749 BC?

    a.   Mohenjo-Daro, Pakistan

    b.   Monte Alban, Mexico

    c.   Nimrud, Mesopotamia

    d.   Bulgaria, Plovdiv

4. When was the construction of Jewish temple begun in Jerusalem?

    a.   540 BC

    b.   530 BC

    c.   510 BC

    d.   520 BC

5. After AD 632, which of the following religions expanded in Eurasia?

    a.   Islam

    b.   Buddhism

    c.   Shintoism

    d.   Polytheism

6. After the T'ang dynasty, which of the following dynasties were established in China between AD 960 and 1279?

    a.   Qin

    b.   Yuan

    c.   Sung

    d.   Ming

7. When did Emperor Henry VI conquer Sicily?

    a.   1174

    b.   1194

    c.   1114

    d.   1104

8. When did the Mongols invade China?
   a. Between 1211 and 1234
   b. Between 1221 and 1244
   c. Between 1231 and 1254
   d. Between 1241 and 1264

9. After 1860, in Cambodia, which new political centres replaced the old temple cities?
   a. Angkor Wat
   b. Bayon
   c. Phnom Penh
   d. Angor Thom

10. When did Manchus invade China and the Ming dynasty was toppled?
    a. 1634
    b. 1644
    c. 1624
    d. 1614

Answers Quiz 108

1. (d) Between 1438 and 1525
2. (a) Mesopotamia
3. (b) Monte Alban, Mexico
4. (d) 520 BC
5. (a) Islam
6. (c) Sung dynasty
7. (b) 1194
8. (a) Between 1211 and 1234
9. (c) Phnom Penh and other cities along the Mekong
10. (b) 1644

Quiz No 109

1. When did Suleiman the Magnificent, under whom's reign the Ottoman empire became one the world's largest powers, rule?
    a. Between 1566 and 1620
    b. Between 1580 and 1599
    c. Between 1500 and 1526
    d. Between 1520 and 1566

2. Where were the earliest civilisations appear to have developed?
    a. Mesopotamia
    b. Egypt
    c. Harappa
    d. China
    e. All of the above

3. When was Teotihuacan civilization established?
    a. AD 100
    b. AD 1,000
    c. AD 500
    d. AD 1,500

4. When was the island of Crete, the first state in Europe, conquered by Mycenaeans?
    a. 400 BC
    b. 1,400 BC
    c. 1,000 BC
    d. 100 BC

5. After the fall of the Han empire in AD 220 until when China remained politically fragmented?
    a. AD 589

b. AD 559

c. AD 529

d. AD 509

6. By AD 200, settlements of which of the following religions were established in several cities of the Roman Empire especially Antioch and Edessa?

    a. Judaism

    b. Polytheism

    c. Christianity

    d. Mithraism

7. When was the Offa of Mercia ruler in England?

    a. Between 737 and 786

    b. Between 727 and 756

    c. Between 707 and 726

    d. Between 757 and 796

8. In which battle was the last Hohenstaufen prince met defeat and death in Europe?

    a. Battle of Benevento

    b. Battle of Tagliacozzo

    c. Battle of Bouvines

    d. Battle of Calliano

9. When did Nadir Shah invade India and sacked the Delhi sultanate?

    a. 1739

    b. 1719

    c. 1729

    d. 1709

10. When did China occupy Annam?

    a. Between 1457 and 1497

    b. Between 1437 and 1487

c. Between 1407 and 1427
d. Between 1427 and 1457

Answers Quiz 109

1. (d) Between 1520 and 1566
2. (e) All of the above, Mesopotamia by 3,500 BC, Egypt by 3,200 BC, Harappa by 2,500 BC and China by 1,800 BC respectively
3. (a) AD 100
4. (b) 1,400 BC
5. (a) AD 589
6. (c) Christianity
7. (d) Between 757 and 796
8. (b) Battle of Tagliacozzo in 1268
9. (a) 1739
10. (c) Between 1407 and 1427

Quiz No 110

1. When did the Turks capture Nicopolis?
    a. 1366
    b. 1316
    c. 1326
    d. 1396

2. When did Harappa adopt urban civilisation in the Indus valley?
    a. By 2,500 BC
    b. By 1,500 BC

c. By 2,000 BC

d. By 1,500 BC

3. Who were the first people to initiate the transition from hunting and gathering to farming around 8,000 BC?
   a. Inhabitants of North Africa
   b. Inhabitants of North Asia
   c. Inhabitants of North Europe
   d. Inhabitants of North America

4. When did Minoan culture emerge on Crete island?
   a. 2,500 BC
   b. 2,000 BC
   c. 1,500 BC
   d. 1,000 BC

5. When did Rome conquer North Africa after defeating Carthage, the other major power in the western Mediterranean?
   a. 346 BC
   b. 446 BC
   c. 146 BC
   d. 46 BC

6. Which of the following was crucified on AD 29?
   a. Jesus Christ
   b. Saint Peter
   c. Saint Paul
   d. Augustine of Canterbury

7. When did Mongols collapse the Abbasid dynasty and capture Baghdad?
   a. 1358
   b. 1258
   c. 1458

d.   1058

8.   Between 1360 and 1405, who was known for his campaigns?
   a.   Genghis Khan
   b.   Timur
   c.   Zahir Uddin Babur
   d.   Salahuddin Ayubi

9.   Which of these were the new political centres which replaced the old temple cities in Thailand?
   a.   Chiang Mai
   b.   Ayutthaya
   c.   Tambralinga
   d.   Sukhothai

10.   When did Frederick II of Hohenstaufen die which led to fragmentation of Italy and Germany?
   a.   1270
   b.   1260
   c.   1240
   d.   1250

Answers Quiz 110

1.   (d) 1396
2.   (a) By 2,500 BC
3.   (a) Inhabitants of North Africa
4.   (b) 2,000 BC
5.   (c) 146 BC
6.   (a) Jesus Christ
7.   (b) 1258
8.   (b) Timur or Tamerlane

9. (a) (b) Chiang Mai (1296) and Ayutthaya (1350)
10. (d) 1250

Quiz No 111

1. In Mesopotamia, when were the centres of earliest cities, ceremonial complexes, constructed?
    a.   3,000 BC
    b.   2,500 BC
    c.   2,000 BC
    d.   3,500 BC

2. When were the first settlements established in Fiji?
    a.   Around 1,500 BC
    b.   Around 1,100 BC
    c.   Around 1,300 BC
    d.   Around 1,000 BC

3. When was the mystical religion of Tao or 'the Way' spread in East Asia?
    a.   In the 6th century BC
    b.   In the 4th century BC
    c.   In the 8th century BC
    d.   In the 2nd century BC

4. Zoroastrianism spread widely in the Roman empire in the form of Mithraism. Later on, most of the Mithraism areas came under the control of which of the following religions?
    a.   Polytheism
    b.   Christianity
    c.   Judaism

d. Shintoism

5. When did the Battle of Tours happen in which Charles Martel defeated the Arabs?
    a. 752
    b. 742
    c. 732
    d. 722

6. Why is the year AD 622 important in Islamic history?
    a. Conquest of Mecca
    b. Hijra
    c. Death of Muhammad
    d. Umar Ibn Khattab became Caliphate

7. Which charismatic leader of the Mongols gained recognition as supreme ruler and in 1206 took the title Genghis Khan?
    a. Zahir Uddin Babur
    b. Kublai Khan
    c. Timur or Tamerlane
    d. Temujin

8. When was the first Muslim raid on Sicily in Europe?
    a. 827
    b. 927
    c. 527
    d. 627

9. When was Shah Abbas, who managed to regain most of the lost territories from Sunnite Ottomans, ruler of Persia?
    a. From 1577 to 1649
    b. From 1587 to 1629
    c. From 1557 to 1619

    d.   From 1527 to 1609

10. When did the Turks capture Kosovo?
    a.   1379
    b.   1369
    c.   1389
    d.   1359

Answers Quiz 111

1. (d) 3,500 BC
2. (c) Around 1,300 BC
3. (a) In the 6th century BC
4. (b) Christianity
5. (c) 732
6. (b) Prophet Muhammad (PBUH) and his followers
migrated from Mecca to Medina (the Hijra)
7. (d) Temujin (1167-1227)
8. (a) 827
9. (b) From 1587 to 1629
10. (c) 1389

Quiz No 112

1. Where was the earliest of all known civilizations,
Sumer, located?
    a.   Mesopotamia
    b.   Kwazulu-Natal
    c.   Sindh
    d.   Sichuan

2. Who is the founder of Asia's most prevalent religion, Buddhism?

    a.   Pythagoras

    b.   Confucius

    c.   Gautama Buddha

    d.   Mahavira

3. Which of the following are prime Greek historians?

    a.   Herodotus

    b.   Hector

    c.   Achilles

    d.   Thucydides

4. In which of the following centuries many tyrants emerged in Greek states?

    a.   Between 2nd and 1st centuries BC

    b.   Between 3rd and 2nd centuries BC

    c.   Between 5th and 4th centuries BC

    d.   Between 7th and 6th centuries BC

5. When did Saint Paul do his missionary journeys?

    a.   Between AD 86 and 97

    b.   Between AD 66 and 77

    c.   Between AD 46 and 57

    d.   Between AD 26 and 37

6. When did Duke William of Normandy conquer England?

    a.   1026

    b.   1066

    c.   1076

    d.   1016

7. When did Songhai break away from Mali?

a. 1400
b. 1200
c. 1600
d. 1500

8. When was the Borobudur in Java constructed?
a. Between 750 and 820
b. Between 720 and 800
c. Between 780 and 850
d. Between 710 and 880

9. When did Chinese invasion of Mongolia end in the emperor's capture?
a. 1049
b. 1449
c. 1249
d. 1349

10. When did the Ming dynasty restore Korea to vassal status?
a. 1382
b. 1362
c. 1372
d. 1392

Answers Quiz 112

1. (a) Northern Mesopotamia
2. (c) Gautama Buddha
3. (a) (d) Herodotus and Thucydides
4. (d) Between 7th and 6th centuries BC
5. (c) Between AD 46 and 57
6. (b) 1066

7. (a) 1400
8. (c) Between 780 and 850
9. (b) 1449
10. (d) 1392

Quiz No 113

1. Who was the first powerful leader in Mesopotamia to establish hegemony over vast areas including the cities of northern Mesopotamia and as west as Byblos?
   a. Ur Nammu
   b. Sargon
   c. Hammurabi
   d. Ashuruballit II

2. When was the Classic period in Mesoamerica?
   a. Between AD 300 and 800
   b. Between AD 400 and 900
   c. Between AD 200 and 700
   d. Between AD 100 and 600

3. When did Harappan civilization emerge in the Indus valley?
   a. About 1,000 BC
   b. About 2,000 BC
   c. About 1,500 BC
   d. About 2,500 BC

4. The founder of which of the following religions was born in 5 BC?
   a. Islam
   b. Buddhism

c. Confucianism

d. Christianity

5. When did Avars, warlike nomads from Central Asia, conquered the Gaul and the Balkans?

   a. AD 750

   b. AD 250

   c. AD 550

   d. AD 150

6. In Islamic World, Abbasid caliphate was at its greatest extent during the reign of Harun al-Rashid. When did he rule?

   a. Between 796 and 819

   b. Between 766 and 789

   c. Between 776 and 799

   d. Between 786 and 809

7. When did Polovtsy sack Kiev?

   a. 1393

   b. 1093

   c. 993

   d. 1193

8. When was Shahjahan, a Mughal emperor of India?

   a. Between 1627 and 1656

   b. Between 1605 and 1627

   c. Between 1526 and 1530

   d. Between 1556 and 1605

9. What is the other name of bubonic plague which killed around 20 million Europeans between 1346 and 1353?

   a. Black Death

   b. Croup

   c. Lockjaw

d. Quincy

10. When did a wave of rebel movements begin in China?
   a. 1627
   b. 1657
   c. 1667
   d. 1647

Answers Quiz 113

1. (b) Sargon (2296-2240 BC)
2. (a) Between AD 300 and 800
3. (d) About 2,500 BC
4. (d) Christianity, Jesus of Nazareth
5. (c) AD 550
6. (d) Between 786 and 809
7. (b) 1093
8. (a) Between 1627 and 1656
9. (a) Black Death
10. (a) 1627

Quiz No 114

1. When did a new empire emerge from Ur, known as
    Akkadian, expanding from the Persian Gulf to
    Nineveh?
    a. Around 1,500 BC
    b. Around 3,000 BC
    c. Around 2,000 BC
    d. Around 1,000 BC

2. When did the Ming dynasty take power in China?
   a.   1338
   b.   1388
   c.   1348
   d.   1368

3. In which of the following centuries were the Europeans first reached to New Zealand?
   a.   18th
   b.   17th
   c.   15th
   d.   14th

4. Who declared war against Asia Minor in 334 BC with an army of 35,000 men?
   a.   Hercules
   b.   Alexander
   c.   Odysseus
   d.   Achilles

5. Who was the ruler of the Islamic World between AD 634 and 644?
   a.   Ali
   b.   Usman
   c.   Omar
   d.   Abu Bakr

6. When did Oleg unite Novgorod and Kiev?
   a.   882
   b.   842
   c.   832
   d.   822

7. Which Mughal emperor in India annexed Bijapur and Golconda in the south, and Orissa in the east?
    a. Aurangzeb Alamgir
    b. Akbar the Great
    c. Shah Rangeela
    d. Shahjahan

8. Which dynasty was established in China in 1368?
    a. Han
    b. Ming
    c. Tang
    d. Xia

9. When was the second dynasty of China, the Chou, overthrown by the western invaders?
    a. By 71 BC
    b. By 171 BC
    c. By 371 BC
    d. By 771 BC

10. When was the Mycenaean civilization collapsed by the invasion of rebellions or outside attack?
    a. Around 1,500 BC
    b. Around 1,400 BC
    c. Around 1,200 BC
    d. Around 1,000 BC

Answers Quiz 114

1. (c) Around 2,000 BC
2. (d) 1368
3. (a) In the 18th century
4. (b) Alexander the Great

5. (c) Omar Ibn Khattab

6. (a) 882

7. (a) Aurangzeb Alamgir (1656-1707)

8. (b) The Ming

9. (d) By 771 BC

10. (c) Around 1,200 BC

Quiz No 115

1. Until when was the Egyptian empire - which was stretched to few parts of Asia - lasted?

    a.   Around 1,600 BC

    b.   Around 1,400 BC

    c.   Around 1,000 BC

    d.   Around 1,200 BC

2. What does the graphic pottery of the Moche, for which the coast of the central Andes is known, show?

    a.   Religion

    b.   Warriors

    c.   Rulers

    d.   Daily life of his makers

3. When was the script 'Linear A' created in Europe?

    a.   About 1,900 BC

    b.   About 1,000 BC

    c.   About 1,600 BC

    d.   About 1,300 BC

4. Whose dynasty provided 'China' its name?

    a.   Prince Cheng

    b.   Wai Bing

      c.   Mao Zedong

      d.   Deng Xiaoping

5. When was Roman empire collapsed by the Visigoths, the western branches of nomadic groups?

      a.   AD 710

      b.   AD 410

      c.   AD 810

      d.   AD 110

6. When did Muslims conquer Jerusalem?

      a.   AD 648

      b.   AD 668

      c.   AD 658

      d.   AD 638

7. When did the building of Great Zimbabwe take place?

      a.   Between 1600 and 1800

      b.   Between 1000 and 1200

      c.   Between 1200 and 1400

      d.   Between 1400 and 1600

8. When did Mughal emperor, Akbar the Great, die?

      a.   1505

      b.   1605

      c.   1205

      d.   1105

9. When was Mongol invasion of Japan defeated?

      a.   Between 1274 and 1281

      b.   Between 1244 and 1251

      c.   Between 1234 and 1241

      d.   Between 1254 and 1261

10. When did Mongols invade Poland and Hungary?

a.   1238
b.   1239
c.   1235
d.   1241

Answers Quiz 115

1. (d) Around 1,200 BC
2. (a) (d) Religion and daily life of his makers
3. (c) About 1,600 BC
4. (a) Prince Chang of Chin dynasty
5. (b) AD 410
6. (d) AD 638
7. (c) Between 1200 and 1400
8. (b) 1605
9. (a) Between 1274 and 1281
10. (d) 1241

Quiz No 116

1. When did the Assyrian civilization arise?
    a.   Around 1,200 BC
    b.   Around 500 BC
    c.   Around 700 BC
    d.   Around 900 BC

2. Under which of the following empires, Gandhara was the centre of images of Buddha, intermingled with Greco Roman influences?
    a.   Hephthalite

b. Sasanian

c. Kushan

d. Achaemenid

3. When did Diocletian become the leader of the Roman world and divided the empire?

    a. AD 484

    b. AD 284

    c. AD 184

    d. AD 84

4. When was the first ecumenical council, the council of Nicaea, held?

    a. AD 325

    b. AD 725

    c. AD 525

    d. AD 25

5. When did the Vikings arrive in Russia?

    a. In the 5th century

    b. In the 4th century

    c. In the 9th century

    d. In the 6th century

6. When was Aurangzeb, a Mughal emperor in India?

    a. Between 1605 and 1627

    b. Between 1656 and 1707

    c. Between 1556 and 1605

    d. Between 1530 and 1556

7. When did Peasants' Revolt happen in England?

    a. 1381

    b. 1388

    c. 1385

    d. 1348

8. Which of the following was a period of civil war in Japan?
    a. From 1477 to 1600
    b. From 1457 to 1580
    c. From 1447 to 1570
    d. From 1467 to 1590

9. When did Satavahanas of the Deccan rule the southern parts of the Subcontinent?
    a. AD 350
    b. AD 150
    c. AD 450
    d. AD 50

10. At the end of a series of civil wars, which collapsed the vast Roman empire, which of these had emerged as a powerful leader?
    a. Caligulus
    b. Tiberius
    c. Octavian
    d. Claudius

Answers Quiz 116

1. (d) Around 900 BC
2. (c) Kushan empire, established by Greeks
3. (b) AD 284
4. (a) AD 325
5. (c) In the 9th century
6. (b) Between 1656 and 1707
7. (a) 1381
8. (d) From 1467 to 1590

9. (b) AD 150

10. (c) Octavian, who adopted the title of Augustus (in 27 BC)

Quiz No 117

1. Who ruled on Assyrian empire after their fall?
   a. Babylonians
   b. Sumerians
   c. Akkadians
   d. Ottomans

2. Which material has been found from the graves filled with funerary offerings of gold and jewellery at Mycenae in southern Greece dating back 1,600 BC?
   a. Plastic
   b. Cashmere
   c. Amber
   d. Silk

3. When were the first farming societies formed in Scandinavia and the British Isles?
   a. Around 6,000 BC
   b. Around 1,000 BC
   c. Around 2,000 BC
   d. Around 4,000 BC

4. When did Huns, nomadic tribes from Central Asia, defeat the Persian empire?
   a. AD 284
   b. AD 484
   c. AD 184

d. AD 84

5. When did Prophet Muhammad (PBUH) die?
- a. AD 629
- b. AD 628
- c. AD 630
- d. AD 632

6. When were the Mongols defeated at Ain Jalut?
- a. 1270
- b. 1250
- c. 1260
- d. 1240

7. When was the Hundred Years' War between England and France happened?
- a. Between 1337 and 1453
- b. Between 1327 and 1463
- c. Between 1317 and 1443
- d. Between 1307 and 1437

8. Who was the founder of the Ming dynasty?
- a. Yu the Great
- b. Chu Yuan-chang
- c. King Wu
- d. Tang

9. Where was 'Minoan' civilization established in Europe about 2,000 BC?
- a. Island of Samos
- b. Island of Patmos
- c. Island of Rhodes
- d. Island of Crete

10. In 1206, who proclaimed Genghis Khan 'universal ruler' of the Mongol tribes?

    a.   Temujin

    b.   Tamerlane

    c.   Kublai

    d.   Babur

Answers Quiz 117

1. (a) Babylonians

2. (c) Amber

3. (d) Around 4,000 BC

4. (b) AD 484

5. (d) AD 632

6. (c) 1260

7. (a) Between 1337 and 1453

8. (b) Chu Yuan-chang (1328-1398)

9. (d) Island of Crete

10. (a) Temujin (1167-1227)

Quiz No 118

1. From where had the earliest written records been found which dated back to 3,000 BC?

    a.   Yellow River

    b.   Harappa

    c.   Mesopotamia

    d.   Mohenjo-Daro

2. During the 6th century BC, which of the following religions originated in Persia?
   a.   Zoroastrianism
   b.   Buddhism
   c.   Shi'ism
   d.   Confucianism

3. When did the Palaiologi empire emerge in the Balkans?
   a.   1241
   b.   1211
   c.   1261
   d.   1201

4. When did Mongols overrun the Chin dynasty?
   a.   Between 1221 and 1244
   b.   Between 1211 and 1234
   c.   Between 1231 and 1254
   d.   Between 1241 and 1264

5. When was the Songhai empire destroyed by Morroccan troops?
   a.   1581
   b.   1571
   c.   1591
   d.   1561

6. When did the Mongols sack Kiev?
   a.   1240
   b.   1210
   c.   1220
   d.   1230

7. When did the Portuguese capture the Malacca in South-East Asia?
   a.   1551

b. 1541
c. 1501
d. 1511

8. When was the Cham capital of Vijaya captured by Vietnamese?
   a. 1471
   b. 1451
   c. 1431
   d. 1491

9. When did one of the rebel leaders capture Peking and the last Ming emperor committed suicide in China?
   a. 1614
   b. 1624
   c. 1634
   d. 1644

10. When was the Shang dynasty flourishing in China?
   a. Between 1200 and 630 BC
   b. Between 1400 and 830 BC
   c. Between 1600 and 1030 BC
   d. Between 1500 and 930 BC

Answers Quiz 118

1. (c) Mesopotamia
2. (a) Zoroastrianism
3. (c) 1261
4. (b) Between 1211 and 1234
5. (c) 1591
6. (a) 1240
7. (d) 1511

8. (a) 1471

9. (d) 1644

10. (c) Between 1600 and 1030 BC

Quiz No 119

1. The earliest written records were found from Mesopotamia. How old are those?
   a. 4,000 BC
   b. 3,500 BC
   c. 3,400 BC
   d. 3,000 BC

2. The Ch'in dynasty was overthrown in 206 BC and unified China was transferred to which dynasty?
   a. Ming
   b. Han
   c. Yuan
   d. Tang

3. When did Muslim Arabs defeat China at Talas river?
   a. AD 751
   b. AD 741
   c. AD 761
   d. AD 731

4. In 1398, who invaded India and sacked Delhi?
   a. Zahir Uddin Babur
   b. Ghiyath al Tughlaq
   c. Tamerlane
   d. Ashoka the Great

5. When did The Black Death spread?
   a. Between 1340 and 1346
   b. Between 1356 and 1361
   c. Between 1336 and 1341
   d. Between 1346 and 1351

6. When was Egypt unified under Menes?
   a. 2,500 BC
   b. 3,000 BC
   c. 3,500 BC
   d. 2,000 BC

7. Who were forced to migrate to Babylon between 586 and 538 BC?
   a. Jews
   b. Mithras
   c. Hindus
   d. Taoists

8. Who was the ruler of the Islamic World between AD 632 and 634?
   a. Ali
   b. Usman
   c. Abu Bakr
   d. Umar

9. When was Nadir Shah assassinated and Persia suffered a period of anarchy?
   a. 1757
   b. 1747
   c. 1727
   d. 1717

10. Kutna Hora silver mines were present in which area of Europe?

a. Bohemia
b. Baranya
c. Bavaria
d. Banat

Answers Quiz 119

1. (d) 3,000 BC
2. (b) The Han
3. (a) AD 751
4. (c) Timur or Tamerlane
5. (d) Between 1346 and 1351
6. (b) 3,000 BC
7. (a) Jews
8. (c) Abu Bakr Siddique
9. (b) 1747
10. (a) Bohemia

Quiz No 120

1. When was the great pyramid constructed by Cheops?
   a. 2,290 BC
   b. 2,690 BC
   c. 2,590 BC
   d. 2,490 BC

2. When did the first Crusade and capture of Jerusalem happen?
   a. Between 1202 and 1204
   b. Between 1189 and 1192

    c.   Between 1147 and 1149

    d.   Between 1096 and 1099

3. Which city became the headquarters of Babur's descendants, the Mughals, in India?
   a. Agra
   b. Delhi
   c. Fatehpur Sikri
   d. Lahore

4. When did east Javanese empire of Majapahit and west Javanese empire of Pajajaran collapsed before Muslim conquests?
   a. In the early 16th century
   b. In the early 18th century
   c. In the early 14th century
   d. In the early 17th century

5. Which of these seized the New World (the Americas) after 1492?
   a. Muslims
   b. Europeans
   c. Hindus
   d. Africans

6. When did Islam begin to flourish in Eurasia?
   a. After AD 634
   b. After AD 644
   c. After AD 632
   d. After AD 655

7. When did the Mongols make their destructive conquests against the Abbasid Caliphate?
   a. Between 1246 and 1250
   b. Between 1235 and 1240

      c.   Between 1226 and 1230

      d.   Between 1256 and 1260

8. Which of these was a centre of Sanskrit culture from as early as the 7th century?
   a.   Palembang
   b.   Plovdiv
   c.   Palermo
   d.   Palmanova

9. When did the inhabitants of Mesoamerica and the central Andes adopt agriculture?
   a.   Around 4,000 BC
   b.   Around 5,000 BC
   c.   Around 6,000 BC
   d.   Around 7,000 BC

10. When was a census done in the Han dynasty of China which revealed around 57 million people living in the empire?
   a.   AD 1368
   b.   AD 2
   c.   AD 484
   d.   AD 242

Answers Quiz 120

1.   (c) 2,590 BC
2.   (d) Between 1096 and 1099
3.   (b) Delhi
4.   (a) In the early 16th century
5.   (b) Europeans
6.   (c) After AD 632

7. (d) Between 1256 and 1260

8. (a) Palembang

9. (d) Around 7,000 BC

10. (b) AD 2

Quiz No 121

1. When was Mayan civilization at its peak?
   a.   AD 1000
   b.   AD 800
   c.   AD 400
   d.   AD 600

2. Around 300 BC, how many states were competing for authority over China?
   a.   7
   b.   10
   c.   15
   d.   17

3. When was Moscow first ever mentioned?
   a.   1167
   b.   1107
   c.   1147
   d.   1177

4. When did Mughal emperor Aurangzeb Alamgir die?
   a.   1656
   b.   1707
   c.   1605
   d.   1627

5. Which of the following centuries were the Europeans first reached to Australia?

    a.   In the 12th century

    b.   In the 16th century

    c.   In the 14th century

    d.   In the 18th century

6. Which of the following is prime comedy Greek playwright?

    a.   Aristophanes

    b.   Sophocles

    c.   Euripides

    d.   Hippocrates

7. Which of the following religions was the first to spread to China by the Ist and 2nd century AD?

    a.   Taoism

    b.   Shintoism

    c.   Buddhism

    d.   Confucianism

8. When did the last Hohenstaufen prince meet defeat and death at the battle of Tagliacozzo in Europe?

    a.   1268

    b.   1258

    c.   1238

    d.   1248

9. When was Lindisfarne sacked by the first Vikings raid in England?

    a.   783

    b.   773

    c.   763

    d.   753

10. Which of these invaded China between 1211 and 1234?

    a.   Abbasids

    b.   Vikings

    c.   Mongols

    d.   Persians

Answers Quiz 121

1. (c) AD 600

2. (a) 7

3. (c) 1147

4. (b) 1707

5. (d) In the 18th century

6. (a) Aristophanes

7. (c) Buddhism

8. (a) 1268

9. (a) 793

10. (c) Mongols

Quiz No 122

1. How many Maoris were inhabiting in New Zealand when Europeans first arrived in the 18th century?

    a.   Up to 150

    b.   Up to 1500

    c.   Up to 150,000

    d.   Up to 15,000

2. Which of the following countries was invaded by the Muslims in AD 711?

a. Spain
b. Germany
c. France
d. Britain

3. Around 1700, after the death of which Mughal emperor several frontier provinces split off from the empire in India?
   a. Akbar the Great
   b. Mohammad Shah Rangeela
   c. Aurangzeb Alamgir
   d. Nasirudin Mohammad Humayun

4. When were the Bantu speaking settlements stretched southwards in Africa?
   a. By 450 BC
   b. By 750 BC
   c. By 650 BC
   d. By 550 BC

5. When did Visigoths defeat the Romans at Adrianople?
   a. AD 78
   b. AD 178
   c. AD 578
   d. AD 378

6. When did Muslims split into the Sunnis and the Shiites?
   a. AD 660
   b. AD 644
   c. AD 634
   d. AD 656

7. Under whose leadership the Mongols first invaded the Chin empire in north China and then turned against the Islamic states to the west?
   a. Mongke Khan
   b. Kublai Khan
   c. Genghis Khan
   d. Timur

8. Which of the following religions was conveyed to humankind through the book Koran?
   a. Hinduism
   b. Islam
   c. Buddhism
   d. Taoism

9. When did Rurik the Vikings occupy Novgorod in Russia?
   a. 862
   b. 892
   c. 802
   d. 812

10. When was the first great Indian civilization established in the Indus valley?
    a. Around 2,000 BC
    b. Around 2,500 BC
    c. Around 1,500 BC
    d. Around 3,000 BC

Answers Quiz 122

1. (c) Up to 150,000
2. (a) Spain

3. (c) Aurangzeb Alamgir

4. (d) By 550 BC

5. (d) AD 378

6. (d) AD 656

7. (c) Genghis Khan (1167-1227)

8. (b) Islam

9. (a) 862

10. (d) Around 3,000 BC

Quiz No 123

1. When is the date of crucifixion of Jesus Christ?
    a.   5 BC
    b.   AD 29
    c.   AD 39
    d.   AD 35

2. When was the Indus civilization of Harappa and Mohenjo-Daro formed?
    a.   Between 3,500 and 2,750 BC
    b.   Between 2,500 and 1,750 BC
    c.   Between 2,000 and 1,250 BC
    d.   Between 1,500 and 750 BC

3. Who was Aurangzeb?
    a.   Son of Mughal emperor Babur
    b.   Son of Mughal emperor Akbar
    c.   Son of Mughal emperor Humayun
    d.   Son of Mughal emperor Shahjahan

4. When did Lithuania, the last remaining pagan state in Europe, convert to Catholicism?

     a.   1327

     b.   1347

     c.   1387

     d.   1367

5. When did Prince Cheng of Ch'in, whose dynasty gave 'China' its name, come into power?

     a.   AD 484

     b.   AD 221

     c.   221 BC

     d.   484 BC

6. Which of the following religions was the first to spread to Korean peninsula by the 4th century AD?

     a.   Buddhism

     b.   Shintoism

     c.   Taoism

     d.   Confucianism

7. When was farming of rice started off in Southeast Asia?

     a.   Around 5,000 BC

     b.   Around 7,000 BC

     c.   Around 3,000 BC

     d.   Around 1,000 BC

8. When was the former Han dynasty flourishing in China?

     a.   Between AD 125 and 320

     b.   Between AD 25 and 220

     c.   Between AD 225 and 320

     d.   Between AD 425 and 520

9. Who was the ruler of the Islamic World between AD 656 and 661?

     a.   Ali

b. Usman

c. Umar

d. Abu Bakr

10. In 490 BC, Greeks defeated Persians in which of the following battles?

a. Battle of Thermopylae

b. Battle of Marathon

c. Battle of Salamis

d. Battle of Plataea

Answers Quiz 123

1. (a) AD 29
2. (b) Between 2,500 and 1,750 BC
3. (d) Son of Mughal emperor Shahjahan
4. (c) 1387
5. (c) 221 BC
6. (a) Buddhism
7. (c) Around 3,000 BC
8. (b) Between AD 25 and 220
9. (a) Ali Ibn Talib
10. (b) Battle of Marathon

END

Reference:

Wikipedia

BBC

The Guardian

New York Times

The Times: Concise History of the World

Printed in Great Britain
by Amazon

21999457R00199